About the Author

Shivaji was born in the latter years of the 1940s, just after India gained her independence from the British Empire. He was named after a great Maharashtrian nobleman and grew up in the central part of the Deccan plateau in the state of Maharashtra, India. Born into a farming community, he was fortunate enough to be given a good education and become a doctor, the first in his family's history. In 1973 he came to the UK to train as a surgeon and while training, met his wife, Heather, and settled as a general practitioner in Lancashire, England. After forty years' service in the NHS, he retired and was soon joined by his wife. They have two grown-up children and grandchildren. He can now be found wandering the lanes around the Ribble Valley or working towards getting his political voice heard.

A Doctor's Journey

Dr Shivaji Devrao Jadhav
MBBS, FRCS, RCPS

A Doctor's Journey

Olympia Publishers
London

www.olympiapublishers.com
OLYMPIA PAPERBACK EDITION

A CIP catalogue record for this title is available from the British Library.

ISBN: 978-1-80074-233-8

This is a work of creative non-fiction. The events are portrayed to the best of the author's memory. While all the stories in this book are true, some names and identifying details have been changed to protect the privacy of the people involved.

First Published in 2022

Olympia Publishers
Tallis House
2 Tallis Street
London
EC4Y 0AB
Printed in Great Britain

Dedication

This book is dedicated to my children, Karina and Sam who are precious to me and to my wife and life-partner, Heather. Last but not least our grandchildren who are special to us.

Acknowledgements

First and foremost, I will always be indebted to my parents, who saw the potential in a naughty, little boy and made him the first child in the family to go to school and get that all important first step in life.

A thank you to all the people I have treated over the years, you have taught me so much more than medicine.

I would like to say thank you to my wife for proof reading and making corrections and without her, I would not have been able produce this book. I would also like to thank Lucy Fishwick for typing my rough draft which must have been very difficult to read. I would also like to say thank you to Olympia Publishers for their support. I am grateful to Christine Hutchinson — for reading through for me and her valuable contributions.

My final thanks go to all my past loyal, hard-working and dedicated staff, without their help I would not have been who I am today.

INTRODUCTION

On the 5th of July 1973, when the Air India 747 aeroplane landed at Heathrow Airport, little did I know I would never return to the land of my birth to live.

I started the early part of my journey and adventures in India. During that period, I had some wonderful times, some scary and some very sad as well.

When my British journey began, I did not know what to expect, but I had more adventures, ups and downs and many happy times also.

I did not think anyone could disown their flesh and blood for their pride and personal prejudice, yet the prejudice was so strong I did not see my in-laws for almost ten years. On the other hand, I did not know I would develop a close bond, which would help thousands of patients.

Finally, when I retired and left my practice after forty years of NHS service, twelve years as a surgeon and twenty-eight years as a GP, my staff and I shed some tears, because they knew, and I knew life would never be the same for them and me and subsequently it proved to be the case. It did not matter that I was a coloured man from a foreign land. It did not matter they were white females born and brought up in UK and it did not matter I was Hindu, and they were Christians. We broke all the barriers and boundaries and developed a human bond with one purpose, to help patients and I knew they would do their best and they did, and they knew I would do my best and I hope I did too. Between us we developed one of the best practices in East Lancashire and were nominated for one of the best practices by our local clinical commissioning group at the time. Together we helped thousands of patients and I hope and pray the Government will preserve and protect that best British Institution, the NHS, because it is the envy of the world.

INDIAN JOURNEY

My Father's Farm and the Early Days

My paternal family were farmers. They had farmed for generations, mainly to be self-sufficient rather than for profit, and they were a very well-respected part of the society. The family was based at Kumtha near a town called Udgir, which was in the southern central part of the state of Maharashtra, India.

My father, Devrao Jadhav, told me about both my grandfather, Atmaram, and great-grandfather, Yogaram. He talked of how they owned two farms, one near to the village and the other a mile away. The one that was close to the village was more productive and well managed.

My grandfather had two children, my father and his younger sister, who unfortunately died at a young age. I never met my grandmother, she died when my father was quite young. My grandfather, Atmaram remarried and had two more sons. From my understanding, my father was the one who worked very hard to look after the farms, but the other sons didn't really contribute or show much interest. Sadly, one of the brothers died of tetanus, in his twenties, the reason I know this was because of the classic description of symptoms and signs of tetanus my father described to me. They were self-sufficient farmers, but you need to look after the farm well, otherwise you cannot make a living. It is twenty-four-seven job. They used to employ workers to help run the farm, later on they sold the distant farm, and relied mostly on the local farm.

My father married my mother, a local farmer's daughter. I do not think her side of the family were well off. My maternal grandfather was called Dhondiba Patil. He had three children. The eldest was a son called Laximan and there were younger twin sisters, this was my mother and her sister. They were called Bhaga and Ganga, named after two Indian rivers, Bhagriti and Godawari, I think those rivers joined together. My maternal grandmother died either during the birth of the twins or soon after, I am not entirely sure. My mother's brother turned out to be not so hard working, and I do not think he did very well for himself. Growing up, I did not see much of my mother's side of the family.

I was the first-born son, and my parents named me after the famous warrior, Chhatrapati Shivaji Maharaj. Shivaji Bhonsale was an Indian warrior king and a member of the Bhonsale Maratha Clan. He was born in 1630 and is renowned for forming the Maratha Empire, being crowned as the Chhatrapati of his realm at Raigad in 1674. Jadhavs are part of the proud warrior caste and as such I was given the honour of bearing his name. Later the airport in Mumbai was renamed after him (and me). However, I am not alone, Maharashtra has many Jadhavs and a plentitude of Shivaji's, in fact is like John Smith in the UK!

I had been born into what could be considered a young country, a new democracy. India had lived under British rule since 1858 and it was 1947 when Nehru led India back into independence. For us this was something that was happening miles away in another land. We had little contact with the outside world, radios were a rarity as was printed news. Our information came from travellers passing through but as the roads were undeveloped this was limited. Growing up where I did, the outside world meant very little to me.

One of the things I remember from a very young age, about my father was that he told me that I must work hard, be honest, treat people better than you treated yourself and never cheat. He also taught me my times tables. I mention this because I passed this onto my daughter, I used to teach her times tables while driving her to her first school, Westholme, in Blackburn.

I was born into a farming community, near a small town called Udgir in the Maharashtra State of India. The capital is Mumbai, it used to be called Bombay, it was changed during the time of the British Empire but is now called Mumbai again. Our place is on the Deccan Plateau — this is an area of flat farming land in central India, more towards the South than the North. My family goes back four generations that I am aware of. It probably goes back hundreds of years, all stayed at the same place and farmed. I was the only one who left our place.

I have one sister, G, she still lives very close to our old place with her extended family. As a boy, I was given priority, my sister didn't get the same opportunities, back then girls were not given the same chances as boys. She was married at probably age sixteen in an arranged marriage with a dowry. This was normal and proper in our society.

My father told me I was very bright, therefore I was pushed up two classes in primary school, meaning I was both the youngest and smallest in the class. I never knew this until later on in my life when my father told me. Back in the late 1940s, in rural India births were not registered and the dates were not considered important, my father calculated my date of birth to the best of his knowledge. What was important was I was born on a Monday, this had astrological significance?

Being the youngest in the class obviously had some disadvantages, especially in sports, but I never let this stop me. I remember getting very frustrated, whenever I came home during the holidays, I used to complain about it. I was very naughty and mischievous in my childhood years. On one occasion my father told me not to go and swim in a river nearby, but when you're with other boys and they tell you your father will be away on the farm and won't find out, foolishly you believed them. On one such occasion I ignored my father and went swimming in the river, bearing in mind I never had lessons. I had a great time with my friends just being boys, having fun. I returned home pleased with my exploits, my father was waiting in the hall. I saw his red face and I realised someone must have told him.

He spoke to me with an unusually stern voice, "Can you remember I told you not to swim in that river, because it is dangerous, and you still went, did you not?"

I was terrified and could not speak, next thing I knew, he brought out a very flexible branch which he used with good force to hit me so hard around my upper abdomen and lower chest. It left angry red marks which stung for days afterwards. I was upset and angry at the time but when I saw the look on my father's face, he was very upset himself and tried to hide his tears from me. I could see it clearly after I calmed down, I realised he was probably more upset than me. I never felt any animosity towards him, he was just trying to protect me. Being an adventurous, fun-loving child, this did not stop me doing other things, like jumping in the wells. I was good at swimming and loved going under water and holding my breath for long periods. We boys liked to go playing around wells. Wells were common on the Deccan plateau the majority of our water came from underground, artesian wells. There were few reservoirs, and there was only the wet season rains to fill them. Being a hot region, water quickly evaporated and refused to stay where the government wanted it! Some years rain didn't come, it was an unreliable water source, but the rain which had fallen on the plateau immediately seeped down through the porous rocks and formed vast underground reserves. We used the water in many clever ways, following the practices of our ancestors so our trees thrived, and our crops survived mostly. We used wells and channels and irrigated our crops using centuries old technology, which had kept this region alive for as long as people had farmed there.

So, the wells fascinated us young boys. I remember one time someone dropped keys in a well and asked me to find them, and I did. The water was very clear, bright mid-day sun was shining on the water and I could see the floor of the well, it was easy for me to jump in, and dive down. I came up to cheers from my comrades. On another occasion someone lost a metal pot in a well. The pot had a wide body with a narrow neck, it had filled with water and sank quickly to the bottom. Yet again, I was asked to get it and of course I was very proud of being asked and did not see or think of any danger. I jumped in, found the pot but with it being full of water, I found it difficult to bring up, so I put my foot inside the narrow neck and tried to swim up but then I couldn't get my foot out and panic set in, then it became a struggle due to fear. Somehow, I managed to get my foot out of narrow neck of the pot and felt very relieved. It was a close call! Thankfully, my father did not know anything about this escapade, and he never hit me again and I always had a lot of respect for him and his stick.

One of my earliest memories is having a fear of snakes. We used to regularly see and hear of deaths from snake bites. We did not live near jungle regions so large cats were not a problem. There was no treatment for snake venom, and in our region there were a number of poisonous snakes like cobras.

One day I was walking on the farm and enjoying myself looking at the scenery. All of a sudden, a large cobra darted straight towards me. I turned and ran for my life. Looking back, I do not think it was going to bite me purposefully, I just happened to be in his way. Even now I have a snake phobia

In my childhood, I had a lot of freedom, I used to climb trees, playing hide and seek on our big mango trees and in the fields, but this I could only do when I was home. The school I went to was strict and young me did not like that part, but it taught me discipline and gave me a good education, which I was grateful for.

I remember the words of a buyer, a travelling business man, who used to buy produce from local farmers and take it to market to sell. I was nine or ten years old at the time. One day, while he was doing a deal, he looked straight into my eyes.

He said to my father, 'Your son is going to England and will become a surgeon — FRCS.'

This guy had no formal education, none of his family were educated either, all he would do was buy farm produce and take it to the market to sell and make a profit. All of his family were involved for generations as far as I know, like my family having been farmers for at least two hundred years. That's what my father told me.

Another incident happened one summer, and I remember it well, I think I was eight or nine. One night, after dark, I was walking on the farm with my father. We stopped under a big mango tree which grew there. My father told me not to be frightened if this particular mango tree shook violently, because it had a friendly ghost, and he wouldn't do any harm. It was a clear night with a big full moon hanging low in the sky. In India we don't believe the moon is made of cheese, or that a man's face can be seen on it. We say there's a deer on the moon. It looks a bit like the Babycham logo, once you see it, it will make sense! On this particular evening there was no wind at all, it was very peaceful. As my father spoke, the mango tree did shake quite violently and a few very green, berry-sized mangos fell on the ground, then it stopped suddenly, and all was still again. It was a mystery, I cannot explain much like the buyer, foretelling I would travel to England and the FRCS. At the time I did not know what the FRCS was, neither did any one of my family or friends. I will explain this later on.

Another childhood memory that changed my life and left a lasting impression which I have always carried with me, was when I was playing in the fields with my friends. One friend in particular I got on really well with, he was quite funny, and we used to laugh a lot together. Once I asked my parents if I could bring him home for a meal. My parents looked at me surprised and thought about it, and then my father explained everything in a calm manner. He said, we have nothing against your friend, but he cannot sit next to you or eat with you, but he can sit away from you on a mat and use a plate, but we cannot use that plate again. We will leave his plate for the next time he comes in. I was a little confused and asked why he could not sit and eat with me? My father was very sympathetic and said that it was not him but the rules of society that were preventing him from eating with us. Then he went on to explain how the whole caste system works. My friend was an Untouchable (Harijan), Mahar in our Marathi language. Harijans eat meat but in Hinduism, which is my religion we do not eat meat. When an animal on the farm like a cow or buffalo died, Harijan people come and collected its carcass, cut up the meat and separated the skin, sometimes they would eat the meat and the skin was given to the shoemakers, known as chambar in Marathi. The term Harijan was first used by Mahatma Ghandi in 1932 when referring to Dalits or untouchables. Harijan means 'Children of God'. He used the word Harijan to bring the untouchables closer to God and there-by also those who believed in God. This was the best of Hindu society.

There were other people in society who did different jobs:

Lohar — these people make farm equipment and metal tools.

Kumbhar — people who make pottery and other things like utensils.

In the caste system, Brahmins are the highest in order. They were often priests and arranged prayers, called puja in Marathi. They used to come to our house and take money and raw materials from us and cook their own food and we cannot touch them or their food, but they gave us blessings on special occasions like weddings.

We were second in the order of the caste system. Being Hindu, we did not eat meat, fish or eggs. Our diet was totally vegetarian and mostly from own farm produce. The only thing we used to buy was salt and clothes. One of the other things we used were dairy products. Every day we had either yogurt, ghee, butter or the liquid which remains after making butter called tak, this was very bland, but spices could be added to it to make a dish called kadi which can be eaten with roti, rough bread or chapati and rice.

This was explained to me properly, along with the caste system and how it worked. I was not very happy with this Untouchable or Harijan bit as my friendship was affected by it. Having observed over the years my parents were not prejudiced at all. My father was a very generous, peaceful and loving man. His belief in Hindu gods was total and he followed the principles of Hinduism well in my opinion. His advice to me was you should treat people better than yourself. Of course, in practice, this can be difficult.

My School at Sirur Tajband
Sirur Tajband is a major village in Ahmadpur taluka of Latur district in Maharashtra. I was about seven or eight years of age when I went away to school. At school, the classes were small, probably twenty in a class and there was very strict discipline, regarding everything cleanliness, punctuality and homework. Teachers were well respected but there was no emotional bond I can remember, they seemed distant. There was lot of sport which was not easy for me as I was smallest in the class, but I still did my best. The two sports I liked best were, kabbadi, which is an Indian wrestling game and running. I hated the discipline, I was rather rebellious, but I survived. One good thing about this school is that I got very good grades and that helped me to go to one of the best colleges and progress further. The school I went to does not exist anymore, I tried to go and see it, but it had been demolished. Now it has been taken over by a different organisation which has schools all over the state.

Pre-Professional College

Throughout my school and university education, I played sports, such as, volleyball, badminton, table tennis, kabbadi and wrestling. In school I got good grades and got into the science college in a place called Nanded.

My two years at college in Nanded were eventful. The first year I was in a larger class. Most of the students in the other class were from families whose parents were either teachers, doctors or other professional people, who knew how to get the best for their children. I was one of the few from the farming community and had no educational background in my family. I was the first one ever to leave home and go to university, somehow, I managed to get good enough grades to get in to second year.

In the second year, you had to make a choice, either you study engineering or medicine. I had achieved good grades in both subjects, maths 90% and science over 65%. The minimum requirement was 60%. It was a difficult decision to make, being totally vegetarian meant that dissecting rats, frogs and other animals not very appealing. However, in engineering you have to do a lot of mechanical work, at least that's what I thought, but I was wrong on that score, you can do various branches of engineering. I had this noble idea if I did medicine, I would at least be able to help people and at the same time I thought if I did medicine, especially when your hormones are showing signs of manhood, I might meet a beautiful young doctor and fall in love. Of course, that did not happen, it was Fate, I will explain that later.

I decided to do medicine, the class was called PPC — a pre-professional course and was quite small, but the lecturers we had were excellent. The lecturers were mostly from southern India. At the time, those states were ahead in education compared to our state, especially the part of the state called Marathwada, where I come from. Marathwada includes five districts. Nanded, where I completed my two years at pre-university college, Aurangabad, where I spent five and a half years at medical school, as well as Latur, Beed and Perphani.

Medical College — The Best Years of my Life.
Entrance to medical college in Aurangabad was difficult. It was the only medical college in the whole region and only had an intake of 100 students per year. Out of that hundred, only sixty places were for higher caste students, like myself, and forty were reserved for the Harijans and the various groups of so-called lower casts, this included sub-castes. This was arranged on the basis that Harijans were underprivileged and they had to compete amongst themselves. From what I knew, at the time, they could get admission with much lower grades than we did. Back then, I felt as though this was unjust but as I grew older, I realised I was being selfish, they deserved to be supported.

There was a total of five thousand applications for a hundred places, only sixty for us upper-caste students in medical school, so for me this was quite concerning as it was uncertain as to whether I would get a place. I think I just managed to get in, which was quite scary. At one stage, I was planning to go to veterinary college if I did not get in. Fortunately, I did not have to, it was my fate to go to medical school, as I had believed from a young age.

Part One of Medical School
The course to become a medical doctor was split into three sections, each lasting eighteen months, but I refer to each part as a year.

Life in my first year of medical school felt rather strange in the beginning. The medical college building was a large, multi-storey and unattractive in my eyes, there was not much greenery around at the time. I always liked green fields, trees, flowers and nature in general. It was a new college and they planted lots of plants and in due course it grew. As it happened, even during my final year the plants had grown, and the garden looked fine.

My accommodation at the college was a single room in a hostel within the college grounds. There were two hostels, one for the ladies and one for the men, about a quarter of a mile apart. There were residential quarters that were used for other teaching staff.

There was a strange tradition in the student hostel in that the senior students had power to influence first year students. Senior students would knock on the first-year students' door and ask them to get undressed. Then they were instructed to tie a rope around his genitals and then while holding the rope in his own hand, he had to go to every room on that floor and salute the occupants. The idea was that you got used to the human body, which you are going to study and dissect from head to toe, during anatomy lessons. Now this is called hazing. It was all well and good but at seventeen or eighteen years old it is quite embarrassing. You could escape this torture if you were friends with any of the senior students. I was lucky enough to be friends with one of senior students and avoided the humiliation.

At the end of the first term, we had a holiday, and I went back home, but by this time I was not really homesick as I had found new friends and was quite happy at the college, but it did not mean I did not want to see my old friends and family.

While I was home, I found out some very sad news, one

of the boys I knew had died, aged eighteen. He had always been very bold, outgoing and used to get into fights. Most boys stayed away from him except for his "gang". I was told that one night, he and a couple of boys decided to steal a goat from a farmer. There was a part of the field, which was used as a goat pen, it was open but surrounded by an acacia tree fence. Acacia have quite sharp thorns, like needles. When this boy jumped over the fence with his bare feet – he did not wear shoes, many didn't — he was okay, but when he tried to jump back over with the goat in his arms, he landed on a thorn and thorn went into his foot. It started to bleed but he could not make any noise otherwise as he would have woken the farmer. He managed to pull the thorn out, and off he went to cut up the goat and enjoy his goat curry with his friends. This was rather unusual considering he was from a Hindu family and his family did not eat meat, but he was friendly with some Muslim boys, who did eat meat. They enjoyed their feast but within a week or so and he developed what I believed to be tetanus.

Tetanus

Tetanus is a disease caused by a toxin produced by the spores of the bacteria, called clostridium tetani. This is found in soil, dust and animal faeces, when spores enter a deep flesh wound, they reproduce, and produce a powerful toxin. This toxin can cause severe muscle stiffness and spasms, which are major signs and symptoms of tetanus. The average incubation period is ten days, but it can be any time between a few days to weeks. Now we rarely see this disease because of the successful vaccination programmes around the world. We in the UK vaccinate babies against diphtheria, tetanus and pertussis (whooping cough) amongst other diseases. You cannot catch tetanus from another person, only from the dirty soil. The main problem with this disease is that it affects your ability to breath due to a powerful muscle spasm of the upper airways, known as lockjaw, and treatment was very basic at the time, now it has improved. This boy was taken to the district hospital, but they could not do anything for him, so he was sent home to die. I was told the end was very tragic, he knew he was going to die, and started pleading with his parents saying, "Please don't let me die, I don't want to die." I cannot imagine how hard it must have been to lose your eighteen-year-old child, and nothing could be done about it. I was personally quite traumatised, and still remember after all these years.

In my final year at medical school, we had to attend the infectious disease wards, and I have seen a number of diseases, diphtheria, polio, tetanus, rabies and tuberculosis, which was common at the time. I did not see any of these in my career as a general practitioner, perhaps tuberculosis and rarely we still see rabies from animal bites in effected countries.

Diphtheria

Diphtheria is disease caused by a bacteria called Coryne bacterium diphtheriae. Now, we do not see this often because of the vaccination, but in places like Africa and India there are still some cases. It is spread by droplet infection, person to person contact or through the air and surfaces the droplets settle on, then if a person touches it and transfers the infection into their body. It takes two to seven days after exposure to show the signs and symptoms, a high temperature, sore throat and swollen neck glands. If left untreated, it can lead to death. It affects the airways, due to tissue destruction in the throat and swelling and a grey/white pseudomembrane, it can obstruct breathing. I have seen little children with this in India, and a tracheostomy was required. This bacterium can also cause myocarditis, which is an inflammation of the heart muscle and can lead to an irregular heart beat and heart failure. Another area affected is the nerves, in particular the cerebral nerves coming from the brain, and paralysis of the area the nerve supplies. How fortunate we are, childhood vaccination has prevented this disease in most parts of the world. This bacterium can be treated with erythromycin or benzypenicillin antibiotics. I only saw one case in England

There were two groups of students in our medical college. One group was from the farming and labouring communities and the other were those whose parents had a higher education, they were either, lecturers, teachers, doctors, professors, judges. One of the student's father, was assistant dean of the college. There were no problems in these groups, just like-minded people getting together and eventually becoming lifelong friends. Even fifty years later I am still friends with one or two of them and there was not a total clear-cut division really. Most of us got on well except for the occasional problem.

During the first year, we had two main subjects to study, human anatomy and human physiology. Our Anatomy professor was trained in the UK and had qualified as a FRCS, Fellow of the Royal College of Surgeons. Our Physiology professor was trained in America and held an American qualification.

Anatomy is the study of every organ, muscle, bone, joint, tissue, nerve and so forth. We had to dissect a human body from head to toe, part by part. We worked in pairs, two students at the head and two at the foot end of the body. Later we swapped over so that we studied the whole body. As you can imagine, for a Hindu boy who had never touched meat, the smell of old flesh and formaldehyde, could leave you feeling very sick, especially at meal times. It was horrendous at first but of course, you get used to it. Formaldehyde was used to preserve bodies

Physiology is the study of how the human organs work together, so that we as human beings, function. I describe some of these as stations in human body as we were taught.

BRAIN — The thinking station, it controls emotions, anger also kindness and caring. It also has influence on many vital functions of organs.

HEART — The pumping station, it pumps oxygenated blood to all parts of your body.

KIDNEYS — The dumping station, it removes all the toxic waste produced by the body which passes to the bladder and into the toilet. Kidneys also convert pro-renin into renin, which subsequently has a role in blood pressure control.

LUNGS — The gas exchange station, takes oxygen from the air and transfers it into the bloodstream and it is carried to the left side of the heart. The lungs take carbon dioxide from blood from the right side of the heart and transfers it to the air. Then plants take carbon dioxide for photosynthesis and produce energy.

BLOOD VESSELS — The transportation station, transport blood to and from parts of the body. Oxygenated blood is carried from the heart to all parts of the body and returns deoxygenated blood back to the lungs.

LIVER — The chemical station, filters the blood coming from the digestive tract, before passing it to the rest of the body. The liver also detoxifies chemicals and metabolises drugs and also acts as storage unit for certain chemicals

BONE MARROW — The defence station, this is a spongy substance found in the centre of the bones. It produces stem cells and blood cells, such as the red blood cells which carry oxygen around the body and white blood cells and immune cells, which defend your body against foreign invaders, like infections.

All these human body stations work well, provided you supply them with oxygen, pure water, healthy foods and minerals, good mental health, but if you do not, you know the end result. I was really glad I passed this part of my examination and was over the first hurdle.

After the holidays, I returned to medical college at Aurangabad, to start my next eighteen months. These eighteen months were the best of medical college life, and no matter what, you are going to be a doctor, therefore, you really begin to enjoy yourself and develop friendships some of which can last most of your life.

Within my group of friends, there were two in particular who used to practically live in my room. I had the same room on campus throughout my university days. Most facilities were shared but I had a decent sized room. My friends lived off campus, one at home and the other in rented accommodation which he didn't like so he mostly slept in my room. This other friend cycled into medical college every day and if he had a free period he would come and sleep on my floor. They had a key each and a mattress to sleep on. One of the friends, was renowned for being careful with money. His parents were quite well off and he was a kind, amiable person, but always tired, he needed his sleep. Every month I received a money order, one time after frequent trips to the cinema, eating out and all the other things I enjoyed doing, by the end of this month me and my not so well-off friend found we hadn't enough money to eat so we pooled our coins and bought bananas and we lived on those until the next money order dropped! Our tired friend never suffered this problem and being an easy going soul, bought us cups of tea when we cajoled him. One time, we wanted to go to the cinema, but he didn't, he wanted to rest. We waited until he fell asleep and liberated money from his wallet. He never bothered or got angry, he hadn't noticed the money was missing, later on we told him and paid him back. His son now practices ayurvedic medicine and he lives in Aurangabad with his family and several grandchildren running rings around him!

During this period, there were student union elections and our group won both presidency and secretary. I was voted into the post of sports secretary. I don't know why? I know I played a lot of sports, but I was not brilliant at any of them. I think it was more a political decision, having said that, the sport minister does not mean he is good at sport. Anyway, it was a good job, and I had a budget of 2000 rupees, (about £21 in 2020), not a vast amount by today's standard but I could authorise the purchase of sports equipment and kit for the sports played in the medical college. One of the highlights of this period is that I thoroughly enjoyed sport, all aspects of it.

Volleyball was a team game I loved, even though I wasn't tall enough to jump high near the net and smash or hit it down the other side. If you are tall it helps, you do not have to jump as high, but being 5'6", I could not do that. Therefore, I chose to throw the ball up so a taller player could hit it. Our team was selected to represent the college for all the Marathwada area. I think we did well as we came third, considering the amount of time we had to spend studying medicine compared to other colleges.

We also represented the college in an Indian game called Kabbadi. I think we came fourth. Playing individual sports, I used to do wrestling which is based on your level of strength and agility. You won if you could put your opponent flat on his back, stopping all four limbs from leaving the ground.

Second Term at Medical College

My second term at the medical college was more relaxing and there was time to enjoy the college life, but there was always a little hiccup when you're enjoying life. We used to go out in the evening to area called Gulmundi, in the centre of Aurangabad, and have something to eat in one of the restaurants. On one occasion, ten of us went and had a good evening. Those days, everywhere, even in the best restaurants they used to give us glasses of water and the waiters would bring four or five glasses at a time, holding the glasses by sticking their fingers in the glass. Now, thinking back, it makes me queasy, but we didn't think at the time. Two weeks after this particular meal, I started to feel nauseous, I lost my appetite, and my eyes and skin turned an interesting shade of yellow and my urine became dark. I was seen by a professor of medicine and had blood taken for testing, back in 1965-66 there were no scans. They diagnosed me with having Hepatitis A.

Hepatitis A

Hepatitis A is a viral infection, and it is passed on via the faeco-oral route. Generally, it is passed on by poor hygiene practices, such as not washing hands after visiting the toilet and before food preparation, through eating contaminated food, raw or undercooked shellfish and less commonly having anal sex or injecting drugs. This is not the same as Hepatitis B which is mostly blood borne. You don't see it often in this country but if you visit tropical and developing countries you can contract it, but a vaccine is available and very effective. There is no specific treatment for Hepatitis A, but I was put on a drip and given a glucose solution for a few days and advised to rest for a fortnight and eat a low fat and low protein diet. I felt very tired and could not walk any distance for a few weeks even though I was normally a very sporty and active person. After four weeks, I was a lot better and eventually made a full recovery. Occasionally, some people have serious complications, and it causes liver failure, but this is very rare. I have had no problems since, and I am convinced I got it from drinking that contaminated water in the restaurant. When you are young, you do not worry about these things and get on with life and I had a very busy life.

During the second and third year, we took quite a few trips away from college in various groups. One occasion we went to a place called Rajgad, where there is a castle where Chatrapati Shivaji Maharaj, an Indian king, fought against Mughals, who came from Afghanistan via the Khyber Pass and occupied most of India for over three hundred years. Then the British took over and ruled for a hundred and fifty years or so.

On this occasion, I remember a group of us riding bikes up a hill, which was something like thirteen miles in 30°C. I was the first to the top, some achievement I thought. I must say I was quite fit.

Some students really worked very hard studying to get to the top of the class but at this stage I was the opposite. I did the minimum amount of work I could do just to pass so I could get into the final year. Days and weeks were passing fast at medical college, studying and spending time on the playing field. I also used to frequent the college gym. I say gym, it was mainly weight lifting.

Third Term at Medical College — Not All Fun

I was in the third year of Medical College when something profound happened which left an impression on my young mind, at the time, and I still remember to this day. As with the tale of my school mate a Harijan (Mahar) and how Hindu caste system discriminated against him, this is similar but more tragic.

It involves one of the pathology lecturers who was probably in his late twenties. He came from an ordinary working-class family (as we would describe them in this country). In India it was a low caste. I do not know exactly which it was, but it wasn't Brahmin, the highest caste! He was a brilliant student and qualified with a distinction and had eventually got a scholarship to go to America to further his education. While waiting to go he was offered the post of Pathology Lecturer at our Medical School. During this time, he met a medical student and began a relationship and fell in love. She was from the Brahmin caste, her parents were educated and well off, but sadly they did not approve of the relationship. It was common knowledge they loved each other but her parents refused to let her see him. He was heartbroken and I am sure she was too, but in India back then girls did not always have the same chances, like my younger sister.

So, they were forced to stop seeing each other. He was depressed and wanted to talk to friends, he needed someone to confide in. One night, things reached a tipping point. He felt low and needed to talk to his friends. He rang two, one after the other and asked if they would go to the cinema, he needed a distraction. Both friends said they were busy and couldn't make time to see him or go to the cinema. These were the last conversations he had. After a walk, he went to his residence, locked the door and closed the curtains. He had got some equipment from the hospital. He set up an intravenous drip in his arm, then added insulin and scopolamine to the infusion bag. Insulin lowers the blood sugar, when the brain becomes deprived of glucose, its energy source it shuts down. The scopolamine (hyoscine) was to stop him feeling sick. He knew how much insulin to use and sadly his plan worked. The next morning the housekeeper noticed the curtains were closed and the door locked, it was unusual for him to be in at that time in the morning. She could not open the door, so she called the hospital warden who helped force the door open. They were shocked when they got into the room, he lay motionless with the drip in his arm. They knew immediately he was dead. A further examination confirmed that he died of an insulin overdose. It was a tragedy, a young man with a bright future in front of him died because of the stupid caste system. I still remember his face and his mild manners. The saddest part is not just in India but many parts of the world, discrimination exists, and it was something that lit the fire to my beliefs in socialism which shaped my political views.

I thought I should write something about insulin, in memory of my lecturer.

Insulin is a protein hormone, produced in the pancreas by the beta cells. The body uses insulin as a bridge for glucose to get from the blood stream into the individual cell, without it glucose accumulates in the blood, and diabetes occurs. Nowadays it is manufactured and used as a medication to lower the blood sugar in diabetic patients. Insulin was first used therapeutically in Canada by Charles Best and Frederick Banting in 1922 and has been one of the most significant medical discoveries of the twentieth century.

Eventually came the last eighteen months of medical college. These eighteen months were very important. This is where you spent a lot of time studying and learning practical medicine. During the first eighteen months we studied human anatomy and physiology, the next eighteen was pathology, microbiology, pharmacology (medicines). These subjects showed what body organs looked like to the naked eye and under the microscope and how they looked different when diseased. This was to help make a diagnosis in different cases, for example taking a biopsy and looking under a microscope as we did with breast cancer.

In pharmacology lectures, we learned about how chemicals worked on the body to cure infections and many other diseases like diabetes, high blood pressure, heart disease and so on. It was very interesting. I managed to pass this part of the course and entered into the final eighteen months of my time at medical college. This is where it all happens, and you become a young medical graduate.

During this term, we had to study a number of subjects and it is quite stressful, you really get very little freedom, but the subjects were interesting. This included general medicine, general surgery, ophthalmology, gynaecology and obstetrics and preventative medicine. I liked surgery best, although I had no problems with any of the others.

We were now allowed to examine patients and try and

make a provisional diagnosis. One of the things we were taught was how to take a good history, do an examination and try to figure out a diagnosis without any investigation. This was the fundamental building block of good medicine and helped me throughout my career. In any case, apart from blood tests and X-rays there were no more investigations available where we were. There was no ultrasound, computer tomography or magnetic resonance imaging scans. These investigations only began to be used during my surgical training when I was in England. This is one of the reasons I was able to make a good preliminary diagnosis from a history and examination alone.

Thyroid Gland

One such example concerns the thyroid gland, which is situated at the front of the neck, it lies like a horse's saddle over the trachea. This gland has a very important role, producing the hormones: tetraiodothyronine and triiodothyronine. These control how the cells in the body use energy through regulating the metabolism and release of these hormones.

Hypothyroidism is when thyroid makes too little of either hormone. There are many conditions causing hypothyroidism, but I will just mention the main ones:

Autoimmune disorders such as rheumatoid arthritis where your body acts against itself.

Iodine deficiency — Iodine is a key ingredient of the two thyroid hormones.

Hyperthyroidism — the thyroid gland is under the control of the pituitary gland in the brain. Benign pituitary tumours can cause thyroid problems. When the thyroid gland produces too much of either hormone it is called hyperthyroidism, it increases the metabolic rate. This increases the heart rate, blood pressure and causes tremors (shaking), feeling hot and profuse sweating. It can also cause irregular menstrual periods, increased appetite, nervousness, poor concentration, brittle hair and an irregular heartbeat. Nowadays, there are a number of investigations, scans and blood tests to detect the exact cause.

Back in the day, where I was in India there was very limited treatment, but nowadays there are medications to treat these conditions and the gland can be removed totally or partially. However, if the whole gland is removed the patient has to take the hormone, thyroxine for the rest of their life. The reason I have written this is to show how much things have changed in my lifetime. I do not think we go into so much detail in the history because investigations can give all the answers.

Addison's Disease

Another very memorable example of how we used to diagnose without modern investigations is Addison's disease. One of my classmates in medical school had this condition and of course we could not forget, the diagnosis and treatment he received, as far as I know he is still alive.

This is caused by a deficiency of the hormone, cortisol and sometimes associated with aldosterone, another hormone. Cortisol is produced in the outer part of the cortex of the adrenal glands which are situated at the top of each kidney. Cortisol deficiency can be quite serious if left untreated or misdiagnosed. One of the physical signs is the skin becomes very dark, called hyperpigmentation and my classmate was a typical example for this. Patients with severe deficiency can go into shock due to low blood pressure. It is thought Jane Austen died from Addison's disease.

Tuberculosis

In those days one of the causes of Addison's disease was considered to be tuberculosis. Now books don't even mention this because the main cause of Addison's disease is primary adrenal insufficiency. The adrenal glands can be damaged by autoimmune conditions such as thyroid disease, rheumatoid arthritis, illnesses where the body is acting against its own tissues. Secondly, the pituitary gland in your brain cannot produce enough adrenocorticotropic hormone which tells the adrenal gland to release the hormones. The treatment is lifelong, you need cortisol tablets every day, and sometimes aldosterone as well. It is known that sometimes genetics can play a part in this condition and one of the things about seeing illnesses first hand, they stick in your brain, and you never forget. The knowledge I gained about tuberculosis as junior doctor helped me when I was working as medical officer at a health centre in rural India.

Tuberculosis was a dreadful disease back in the sixties. I received a letter from my father, telling me someone from our town was quite ill, coughing a lot and had lost weight. The local doctors told his parents they couldn't do anything more for him. My father asked me if his parents could bring him to Aurangabad Medical College. I said yes, in the meantime, I asked my Professor of Medicine, he said it was fine, but it would have to be as an outpatient as there were no tuberculosis beds in the hospital. When he came, I did not recognise him, he had lost weight, his cheeks were hollowed, he looked pale.

He coughed constantly. When he arrived, I let him stay in my room. A patient with open tuberculosis staying in my room! I do not know how I didn't catch it! Fate? Open tuberculosis means the patient is very infectious. He received streptomycin injections; that was the treatment back then. Sadly, after treatment there was no improvement, and he was allowed to go home basically to die. He died within a few weeks, he was about twenty years of age. It was heart-breaking, now there is screening and treatment, though people in developing countries still succumb due to limited medical resources.

In our final year of medical college, we were allowed onto the clinical wards, to study medicine, surgery, obstetrics and gynaecology first hand.

Rabies

I remember my time on the infectious disease ward vividly. On this ward we were able to see a wide variety of infections we rarely see nowadays. Tuberculosis was common, so was diphtheria, tetanus and rabies. I did see a rabies patient and that was a frightening experience. Rabies is a viral disease, causing inflammation of the brain. It is a virus from the Lyssavirus groups. When an infected animal, often a dog, but could be a cat, monkey or bat, bites you or you come in contact with the saliva of an infected animal and it gets inside the body either through the eyes, nose or mouth, you can get rabies. It typically starts 1–12 weeks after the bite or scratch. The two most striking things about this disease are it causes hydrophobia, the fear of water, and uncontrolled movements when seeing or hearing water and the patient has to be restrained by physical means, but things have changed now, and management is better. I saw several patients with rabies, and it was quite frightening for a young medical student. These days there are rabies vaccines, and it can be treated with immunoglobulins if it is caught early.

The best thing to do with the animal bite is to wash the wound thoroughly with soap and water. In an emergency if no water is available rinse with any fluid, but alcohol is best, preferably over 40% proof. If treated before neurological symptoms develop then recovery is possible, but once neurological symptoms develop it can be fatal.

Finally, it was the final medical examinations, I can't remember exactly but it seemed to go on for weeks. I did pass with good grades, I was very pleased about it, but at the same time a little sad. I really enjoyed all the aspects of my life at medical college and made a number of friends and still to this day I see them when I visit India. I call those days of my education, one of the most carefree, innocent and happiest times of my life.

Now begins the responsibility of being a doctor and saving lives. We had to take the Hippocratic Oath but not quite yet as we have to do a twelve months internship. We used to call pre-registration house officer in UK

The Hippocratic Oath says, "To treat the ill to the best of one's ability, to preserve a patient's privacy, to teach the secrets of medicine to the next generation".

Hippocrates was a Greek physician and although there is some controversy as to when it was written and also what he actually said, "do no harm", is one of the statements in some documents or another description of the oath. The oath is still followed all over the world including, the General Medical Council in the UK and the American Medical Association in America. Certainly, if you do not follow certain principles, you can face disciplinary action or even lose your license to practice, which I have seen happen.

Now I had passed my final examination, but I still could not practice independently until completing one year of internship. This was in the main specialities, medicine, surgery, obstetrics and gynaecology, ophthalmology and preventative medicine. This was a very interesting twelve months, we were actually learning practical skills by taking thorough histories, examination and the limited investigations, there were very few by today's standards, mainly we had X-rays and blood tests and in some cases histopathology. This really honed my basic skills, teaching me to diagnose most conditions with history and examination. Out of all the subjects, I liked surgery the most. Professor M. had been to the UK and had his postgraduate qualification FRCS. He was a good teacher and seemed very strict but fair and I respected him. Of course, all the professors who taught us were fine people, but he just seemed different and left a lasting impression on my mind. To a degree he sowed the seeds of my interest in surgery and my subsequent progress to that specialty. Did I ever think the seeds would ever grow and turn into green shoots and fulfil my ambition to be a surgeon?

Nothing really outstanding happened in the last twelve months, I continued to stay at medical school but started to earn some money, but I had very little time to spend it. I had to work long hours and was always busy.

When I left medical college and thought of the happy times I had there, I also thought about how much I had changed.

Firstly, I'd arrived a Hindu and a vegetarian but turned into a non-vegetarian, eating eggs and chicken. My first thought when tasting chicken was that I liked the sauce or gravy, but I did not think much of the meat. By eating flesh, I had broken generations of Hindu tradition in my family. I always remain a Hindu at heart and remember the times I went to temple with my father and how we celebrated the major festivals, Diwali and Holi.

Secondly, I had started drinking alcohol in my final year at medical college, then more so when I became a medical officer at a primary health care centre. I was well and truly the black sheep of the family, as the saying goes.

In The Army Now!

Something I remembered when I was writing about my experience at medical school, and I thought it's worth mentioning.

I only visited the state of Gujarat from medical school because it was compulsory to do some national army training for a short period during our time at medical college. I think it was maybe once a year. One year we had to go on tour to a forested region and stay in army camp. A few of us, the naughty ones tried to escape during the evenings and go to the nearest town to get something to eat and return without anybody seeing us. Occasionally we got caught and the punishment was a double march. In Indian army terms this meant you had to run a quick mile or so. I am thankful that's all it was because I started to get evening rigors, a shaking, shivering and feeling hot and cold. I told Subhedar, the soldier in charge of our unit. He told me I looked all right, and to just get on with it. He said in the army we do not tolerate soft people. During the day I felt better, so I just carried on for a week.

Another time, two or three of us decided to escape the camp in the evening. I was not feeling that energetic, but we managed to escape to the nearest village. We had something to eat and walked back. That night I had the shivers and hot and cold sweats again and could not sleep, but the next morning I got up and carried on. The next time we tried to sneak out we got caught on the way back and our punishment was a one-mile quick march. I do not know how I managed. I think I had malaria. Malaria can be a quite serious disease and kills thousands of people, especially in Africa.

Malaria

When I said I had malaria in the army camp in Gujarat, I think it must've have been a mild type. There are four types of single-celled malarial parasites, known as: plasmodium vivax, plasmodium falciparum, plasmodium ovale and plasmodium malariae. The plasmodium falciparum is the most severe and a major cause of death in the world. Reports suggest that one child dies every two minutes in the world and there are over 200 million cases reported every year, most are from Africa.

The disease has different phases: When an infected female anopheles mosquito bites, it releases the parasites into the blood stream these travel to the liver where they mature and reproduce. Then the mature microorganisms return back into the bloodstream and into the red blood cells where they multiply. This leads the red blood cells to burst, we call this haemolysis. This causes the classic symptoms of chills, headaches, sweating and a high-temperature. The symptoms come in cycles every two to three days. Some books suggest it takes ten to twenty-eight days for symptoms to appear, my personal experience is slightly different.

When I was a GP, I saw a seven-year-old girl who had travelled to Pakistan twelve months prior to her symptoms developing. There was no history of any other travel other than these twelve months previously with her family, but her symptoms were strongly suspicious of malaria. I arranged a blood test which came positive for malaria. The only alternative explanation I can think of it was "Suitcase Malaria", a mosquito had hitched a lift with a more recent traveller. This may be an exception, but it shows it can happen. I think I must've had one of the milder varieties, and I recovered well.

Subsequently, I completed my training and got my medical degree certificate MBBS, Bachelor of Medicine and Bachelor of Surgery, and now I could practice on my own as a qualified doctor. Finally, I took the Hippocratic Oath. MBBS, sounded very glamorous but I was terrified that I was alone in the big wide world without anyone's help or supervision. The other thing I must mention is that I thought I would fall in love and get married at medical college, which never happened, and maybe Fate meant it that way because someone in the UK was meant for me?

Now I was free to apply for the jobs either in a speciality anywhere in India or as a medical officer at a primary health centre. After some deliberation and seeing a number of doctors were going abroad to gain degrees, mainly in America, and the UK, I decided that was what I would do. For America you had to pass an examination called ECFMG (educational council for foreign medical graduates) but the Indian Government or at least in Maharashtra they were discouraging doctors from going abroad and there was no place anywhere in India you could go for this examination. You had to fly to Kuala Lumpur in Malaysia, so I decided to apply for the UK.

To go to the UK, you did not need an examination, instead you got offered a clinical attachment and were paid during that period. Then, if you completed it successfully you could apply for other jobs. We had to apply at least twelve months in advance and wait. During this period while waiting I applied for a post as a family planning medical officer at a primary health care centre in rural India. I could have applied to better places like Taluka, which is like council headquarters, where there were more facilities and you can earn more money by doing private practice, but most of these jobs were given to doctors who had some political connections, or they paid a "donation". It was corruption in my opinion at the time. I did have political connections, one of my good friends had become a Member of the Legislative Assembly of Maharashtra State. The Legislative Assembly formed the State Government, and the head of this Government was called the Chief Minister. I did not use my political influence as I felt uncomfortable doing so. Therefore, I applied for a job at a primary health centre and was appointed as a Family Planning Medical officer at a place called Koli. This was a rural place with very few facilities. It was near the border of our State, and it was obvious no doctor wanted to go there. When I mentioned to some of my friends, they thought I was mad, they said I could have got a lot better places if I wanted but I had made my decision and I was going to try and do my best.

First job and a thousand vasectomies — Koli Primary Health Care Centre

Koli Primary Health Care Centre, Hadgaon taluka, District Nanded was my next destination. I must explain, a district is like a county. Koli was a small village, and apart from the Health Centre there were no other offices or professional people, it was very much isolated. There were two medical officers, myself and another doctor, a nurse, a health visitor and a receptionist. There was no government accommodation. Most developed health centres, had doctors' accommodation but here we had to find a house and rent it, that was difficult at the time. Anyway, the two of us found some accommodation and only one of us would stay there as required, but the rest of the time we stayed in a government bungalow at Hadgaon, a taluka place, as I explained taluka is the administrative division or headquarters of council offices and it was based at Hadgaon

In the 1970s the Indian healthcare system began with health care centres. These were very basic facilities with little in the way of medication (there were no pharmacies). We had paracetamol for fever and codeine for pain and sometimes penicillin to treat all infections! These health centres provided care for the surrounding area. The role of the health centres was to provide preventative intervention such as family planning, sanitation and basic health advice.

For more complicated illnesses there was Taluka Hospital which used to be called a civil dispensary. It covered a wider area and had more facilities and medication. Next was the District Hospital, this was the largest hospital serving the whole district and had all the major specialities. The Government Bungalow was built for all visiting government officials to stay just for short visits while on official duty. Sometimes we stayed longer than we should if there was no one else staying there.

Like most professional people in India at this time I employed someone to help me, we called them servants. Jamal was his name. Looking back, I have no idea how old he was, he was spritely and hard-working, his face aged by modern standards, heat, dust, physical stress and diet can make a young man age before his time. I think he must have been influenced by Mughal traditions as he was very old fashioned in his mannerisms. Every time he saw me, he used to salute and click his heels together like soldiers did in the army. I used to say, Jamal you do not need to do that, but he just used to smile and did it anyway. He did everything for me, ensuring my clothes were washed and cleaned. He ran errands and arranged food and transport. He was a very gentle, kind person and I will always remember him. When I left there were genuine tears in his eyes. Having a servant was the norm at the time, all households who could afford it had people to help. I was supporting another person and giving him a job and money. He was invaluable to me, and I always carry fond memories of him. When I finally left, I was very emotional also, he has been a part of my journey.

At the government bungalow there was some social life as a number of government officials stayed there on their visits. We used to meet them socially, I became very friendly with one family in particular. They were married couple with three young children, and I almost became part of their family and sometimes stayed at their house. I was very emotional when the time came to leave them, but I had some happy memories to take with me.

The job at the health centre was frequently frustrating. There was very little medication available either at the health centre or outside, there were no pharmacies. Patients came from anywhere nearby and sometimes from quite a distance, often walking miles. I would examine them, mostly I knew what was wrong but because of the scant facilities I could not treat them properly. Poverty in this area was striking. If you wanted to refer them for further treatment, the nearest district hospital was sixty kilometres away. Patients rarely had transport and depended on patchy and not very reliable public transport. On a few occasions I ended up taking them to the hospital myself, but there would be no further communication from the hospital, so we never knew what happened to them.

On one occasion a middle-aged man was brought by cart to the health centre. He had been vomiting and had diarrhoea for a few days and was not getting better. He was brought to the health centre as a last resort. By the time he arrived he was badly dehydrated, his tongue and mouth were dry, his skin looked pale, eyes shrunken, his pulse was rapid and thready, and his blood pressure was dangerously low. In addition, he had not passed urine for twenty-four hours and when he arrived, he was semiconscious. We could not give him oral rehydration; he could not swallow, and we did not have any intravenous drip facilities. I was planning to take him to nearest Taluka hospital at Hadgaon, but before we could put him in our vehicle he arrested and irrespective of our best efforts at resuscitation he died. That was one of the saddest days in my early medical career. It was difficult to apportion blame. The government at the time was a young democracy, it was just over twenty-five years since the British had left India after ruling for one hundred and fifty years. Before that the Mughals had occupied India for over three hundred years. In addition, there was a lot of corruption in the government at the time and I am sure that played some part. I was not a happy man, I started drinking alcohol on a regular basis at Hadgaon, a Taluka place and made some friends there. One thing I noticed about alcohol is that it makes you feel better for short while, but you feel worse after the effect wears off. It was not really the answer, but I did not give any thought to that at the time. My main job at the health centre was family planning. We gave advice and performed male sterilisation, a procedure called a vasectomy and for female sterilisation, a tubectomy. I remember we used to visit different villages where our health promoter would bring large numbers of patients, men generally as the operation is quicker. Our target cohort was anyone who had a minimum of two children, and there was an incentive for the patients, given by the government, usually a radio or some money.

There was this slogan, "HUM DO HAMARE DO" which roughly translates as: "Us two and our two"

I used to do between forty and fifty vasectomies per day during camp season, it was like a conveyor belt. Needless to say, I became very good at vasectomies, I was doing one every fifteen minutes. Being young I had good eyesight and fine motor skills. Complication rates were not recorded, there was no routine follow up. We were simply a cog in the government machinery. We had been given an annual target and had to produce a report. I was not very happy with this, but I was only there for a short time and did my best.

During my time working at the Koli Primary Health Centre I had a Jeep, which I drove everywhere. In India at the time driving licenses and even lessons were not necessary. One day I was driving through a crowded road in Taluka Place and for whatever reason I lost control and ran the Jeep over a fruit and vegetable stall. Luckily, no one was hurt, but all the merchandise was squashed and flattened! I managed to stop, got out and asked the shopkeeper how much the damage was and just paid for it! Now I can see the sheer arrogance and I must say it was not my finest moment and I am now quite ashamed. I did not even say sorry. My only defence, if I have one, was I was young, immature and did not have a lot of life experience! Learning to drive by switching on an engine and just going made it harder to pass my test in the UK as being self-taught, bad habits are difficult to break!

We used to get a visit from our District Medical officer to check our progress and he would stay at the Government Bungalow at Taluka place. This particular medical officer was from Goa, an area called Kokan, and he liked a drink. It was our job to provide him with alcohol and food; maybe that was bribery? I do not know but everybody did the same. He knew I was planning on going to the UK and was there temporarily.

The idea was to go to the UK, get a job and then take the American examination and go to America. The time was going fast and by now I should have heard from the passport office. The Maharashtra State capital was Bombay, now known as Mumbai, and the only place in our state with a passport office. Maharashtra State is one of the largest states in India. I was working about two hundred and fifty miles away in a rural health centre in the district of Nanded. I had applied for my passport through the post office by registered post and I knew they had received it, as one thing about India is that for such a vast country, the post office worked very well. Post usually reached its destination within three days, anywhere in India, this was one of the positive things the British Empire did for India. After waiting three months and having no reply I was getting concerned. I decided to go to Aurangabad, where my medical school friend, M. P. was based. By now, not only was he a doctor but he had become a Member of the Legislative Assembly (M.L.A.). This was part of the Maharashtra State government. As my friend was a M.L.A. he knew how the system worked and had political contacts, as well as having the power to change things or get things done.

When I met him, I told him about how I'd applied for a passport and was planning to go to the UK in six months' time. I explained I had applied three months earlier and not heard anything. Then he just burst out laughing and said, 'That's not unusual because there's a lot of corruption and unless people pay "*gifts*" nothing gets done!'

"Gifts" was a polite term for a bribe. My friend M. P. was usually quietly spoken and a man of very few words. This was a completely new experience for me, and he asked me to accompany him to Mumbai which I did. There he went to the passport office and said to the clerk at the reception he wanted to see the person in charge of the department, but the duty person tried to make excuses. My friend just walked through to the head of the passport department, and I followed. He told the head of the department who he was and asked him why his friend, Dr Shivaji Jadhav, had not received his passport or not had even had a reply? The man tried to make every excuse possible, I could see he was trying to tell lies. Then M. P. told the Officer he wanted the passport to be done as soon as possible. I did get my passport soon after that. At the time I felt very sad and angry for our young Indian democracy. India gained its independence on 15th of August 1947 from the British.

While my preparations were going ahead to go to the UK, I got a letter from the superintendent of Ballochmyle hospital near Glasgow in Scotland offering me a clinical attachment to a surgical consultant. The attachment meant free accommodation and subsidised canteen meals, like all other staff and also a basic minimum wage for about six to eight weeks. Then during this time, if you satisfy the consultant, you can apply for jobs through the British Medical Journal, anywhere in the country.

My father wasn't happy on two counts. Firstly, that I was leaving, without getting married and secondly, he felt I would not come back. Being the only son, I could understand his concerns. He has been told by many people that when doctors go to England, they get married and never come back. He tried his best to get me to marry before I left but I was not ready for it. I explained to him once I got my FRCS, I would be back and told him not to worry. Of course, I did not know at the time, what he said was true, in my case at least. I always believed in fate and that it was meant to happen. My greatest regret was that I was not there to look after my parents in the later years of their life. But when you are young and ambitious, you do not always think of the consequences and in my case, I did not.

Now the time to leave was approaching and I had to get ready, and I was quite excited but at the same time apprehensive. I have never been abroad before. I received a letter for an interview at the British Embassy in Mumbai and was given a date and time to attend. I planned my trip well in advance, I went one day before, just in case and stayed in Mumbai. I am not really a fan of big cities and Mumbai was mushrooming. Aurangabad was quite big but compared to Mumbai it was tiny. I remember this British person with what I considered to be a very different British accent which I was not used to asking me questions. He asked many things, like why I had chosen the UK as part of my education and if I got a job, what would I like to study and how long did I think it will take me to complete. I was very surprised at how clearly he spoke, and for me to understand and he gave me time to answer. I think I was very clear with what I wanted to do, I planned to become a general surgeon, or a second option would be a cardiothoracic surgeon. I said I will probably take three to four years to pass my examination. I was surprised with myself. I was not worried or showed any nervousness although this was in reality make or break for my future plans. There was no Plan B. He also asked me a few more questions about my family and my health. All went well I thought, and I was pleased but not sure if I'll get the job or not, but there was nothing I could do, other than wait. I was told they will inform me and if I get a job, I will need a private medical examination at Breach Candy Hospital in Mumbai, and they will pay for it. I thought that was a very good start from the country I've never been to, and it was very generous of them. I would've paid the expenses if I needed to. There were a number of people waiting to get a Visa to go to the UK, not just doctors but for various other reasons but it was very well organised. Later that afternoon sometime after three p.m. I was told I had been granted permission to go to the UK, to Scotland, provided I passed the medical. The medicals had to then be arranged so I went to the Breach Candy private hospital to make an appointment. It was new experience for me to travel in Mumbai, it was a vast and busy city. The traffic was chaotic, I had never seen anything like this before. I eventually managed to get there and made the appointment. This meant I would have to come back in two weeks, so I went back to my job at the health centre. The staff were very pleased for me, as I got on really well with everyone. Well, I say everyone, there were only a few staff including an attendant, who was to help us with all our daily needs and a driver. All through my working life I have always tried to be friendly with whoever I was working with.

Now, I was just hoping the medical examination would be okay. I don't know what I would have done if I had failed. I reassured myself that I was quite fit and well with all the sport I used to play but I had one bad point from a health point of view, which was how my mind worked at the time. I used to drink almost every evening as there was nothing else to do at this small place and I was a bachelor. So, for the next two weeks I did not drink any alcohol just in case.

Now I was very restless and not enjoying work as much, but I tried to concentrate and do my job. Finally, I went for my medical as usual the day before and stayed in Mumbai. The doctor who examined me was British, pleasant and well mannered. He did a full medical examination and chest X-ray just in case I had tuberculosis which was quite common in India at the time. All went well and he told me there was no problems and he would pass the report to the Embassy, but he told me to keep hold of the chest X-ray and take it with me to the UK, just in case anyone questioned me, but he said there was no evidence of tuberculosis, I keep this X-ray even today. This was good news.

I had another two months before I departed to the United Kingdom. Now I had to plan everything, clothes, foreign currency, but my first priority was to book a flight. My friend was also planning to go to the UK but before he went, he was doing his postgraduate diploma in Ear, Nose and Throat surgery at a hospital in Mumbai. He helped me buy plane tickets through the travel agent. He'd already been in Mumbai for eighteen months and knew all about travel to the UK, he had made a special effort to find out. He was one year senior to me, and I knew him well, he had been the student union president at Aurangabad Medical College. We always got on well, he was one of those people who smiled a lot. He was always very charming and well-mannered to everyone, and he took me under his wing.

At home, my family organised an Indian style party, as Indians do, inviting family, friends and everybody else. It was my last night at home, and it was very emotional for all of us. I never slept that night, the next day I was leaving my family and the farming heritage of at least four generations behind me. I never thought that I would not return to live in India, the UK only a stepping stone in my education. Before I knew it, I was on my way to Mumbai. As I was saying goodbye to every member of my extended family and friends, my father called me to one side and gave me a large gold ring and said if I ever wanted to come home, for whatever reason, I could sell this ring and use the money for a flight. It was just a simple twist of gold, but I kept it with me. Sadly, in 1988 our house was broken into, and the ring stolen.

The Indian government had put restrictions on how much foreign currency could be taken out, especially sterling pounds and US dollars because the government needed the foreign currency, at least that's what I was told. I could only exchange Indian rupees to the value of £43, which is worth about £530 today. I suppose in 1973 the pound was a very valuable currency. I remember, I think a postage stamp was two to three pence then, and a meal in a canteen cost less than a pound, probably about forty to fifty pence. Some people did take more money if they could buy it on the black market, but I just took what was legally allowed and I knew I had a job and would get some wage and free accommodation in the UK.

The next two days I stayed with my friend in his hospital accommodation. We did all the chores and whatever else shopping I needed. I bought two suits, ties and one jacket, shirts, socks and jumpers and filled my half empty suitcase. This was all done with my friend's help. On my last night, he organised a little party with friends who were from our college studying for post-graduation qualifications. The next day, a number of them came to the airport with me and said their final goodbyes. When I left them, it felt really strange. I was on my own and leaving India not knowing how I would cope, even now when I am writing the thought of this time makes me feel quite anxious, I sometimes wonder how I ever managed it.

I climbed those steps of that Air India 747 and left the Indian part of my journey behind for good and that's what happened on the 5th of July 1973.

British Journey

When I climbed those stairs of the Air India plane and waved my goodbyes to my friends who had escorted me to the airport, it was a very emotional moment. Once I got on the plane and sat down, I was so exhausted, I fell sleep and slept most of the way and don't remember much of the journey. I landed at Heathrow airport at about two p.m., and I had about two hours to get through customs and find the domestic terminal for the flight to Prestwick airport near Glasgow.

This was a totally new experience for me, and I had to ask for directions more than once. It was surprising how helpful people were and that was my first impression of British society. I got to the terminal just in time and I was on my way to my destination in Scotland.

1973 — Ballochmyle Hospital

I think I arrived at about six thirty p.m. at Prestwick. It was quite a small airport, this made it easy to get through. From there I got on a bus to Ballochmyle hospital.

Ballochmyle hospital was established in 1939 as one of the seven emergency hospital service facilities for military casualties and it eventually closed in 2000. I arrived at the hospital and found my way to the reception, the staff were very pleasant and helpful, and I was taken to my accommodation.

The hospital was all on one level and my accommodation

was one room with a wash basin, a shower, a toilet and a bed. There was a side table with a lamp next to the bed. It was good enough for my needs and I was very happy with it. All junior doctors were based on this site, and it was a little like a dormitory with a long corridor, just like my medical college hostel. The hospital was just a few minutes' walk away.

On that July evening, the sun was still shining, I had arrived in a beautiful green surrounding. I don't exactly remember but I think I was shown around the facilities such as the dining hall, called the doctors mess, where we would be able to take our meals. I had very little to eat that night and had a very early night.

My surgical clinical attachment was with Mr M, a consultant general surgeon. I think I was lucky as he was very pleasant, quietly spoken and very thorough. His unit had one registrar and he was from Pakistan and had already passed his FRCS and was doing most of the major surgeries independently. We also had two other junior doctors, one house officer and one senior house officer. I was right at the bottom of the pecking order. My instructions were to follow the team, the registrar, senior house officer and house officer and of course, never forget, the sister. My consultant gave me some very important words of advice, always get on with the ward sister and nurses because they have been there a long time and know a lot more than some junior doctors. I never forgot that advice throughout my career and it helped me a lot.

One of my main problems was trying to understand the Scottish accent of the staff and patients. I had to listen very carefully and sometimes asked with an "Excuse me, can you repeat that?" In fairness they probably found it difficult to understand my Indian accent too, but they never said anything.

My daily routine was to get up, have a shower and go to the canteen for breakfast and I think I used to have toast and tea. Then I would go to the ward and join the house officer and senior house officer and follow them around to watch them do various jobs such as taking bloods and wound swabs if they suspected an infection. After the routine specimen collection, we moved onto taking histories and examining any new admissions. Next the registrar used to come and have a ward round with the ward sister and junior doctors. We would see all the post-operative patients and any new emergency admissions. The consultant did one or two ward rounds a week. We all followed him and then carried out any instructions he gave. This was a well organised unit, and it ran very smoothly. Of course, there were complications sometimes, but these were dealt with thoroughly and efficiently. Even now, I feel it was the best system and during my forty years working for the NHS it became a lot busier and kept changing and it became worse rather than better in my view.

As my routine was well established, I was very happy with the way things were going, I was given bit by bit more responsibility as they felt I could cope. After around a month in the job I was asked to take histories and do examinations. Of course, this was checked afterwards by the senior doctors, but I never had any problems with this part of my work. I had applied myself and been taught well in medical school. I started taking blood samples and helping with other investigations. I used to get around £15 a week for this job, food was subsidised, and accommodation was totally free so that meant I didn't spend much money at all. There were some sports facilities including tennis and badminton courts but apart from that we used to spend evenings watching television in the doctors' common room. After four weeks, I was asked to see my consultant, I was very worried because I did not know what this was about. I had no idea, so it was natural to worry but I knew I have not done anything wrong or made any mistakes and nobody said anything untoward to me.

Anyway, I didn't have to worry, it was good news. Mr M. asked me to sit down and made me comfortable. Then he asked me how I was and if I was enjoying my time at Ballochmyle? I said I was absolutely enjoying it. He said he was happy with my progress and now I could apply for jobs in a junior capacity, anywhere in the country but he preferred me to stay in Scotland if I could get a job. I was delighted and I said thank you very much for your kindness and help. I left with lots to think about.

Now the difficult task began! I did not know anything about how the system worked. I asked the senior doctors about how to apply and where to find these jobs? The answer was the British Medical Journal and the BMJ became my friend for the next ten years. Each week there were literally hundreds of jobs advertised all over the country, in Scotland, England and Wales, there were even some abroad.

I started my applications that same evening and there was not much to write on my CV as I had very little experience in the UK really. All the experience I had was in India, in general practice and family planning mainly. I applied for as many jobs as I could, I needed a job, or I would be cashing in my father's gold ring and heading back to my motherland. Fortunately for me, within a week I had an interview at the nearby Stonehouse hospital working as a Senior House officer in the accident and emergency department.

The interview went well and my reference from Mr M was good I think, and I got offered the post. This was my first proper job in the UK. I wrote to my parents to tell them the good news and to some of my friends in India too.

1973 Stonehouse Hospital, Scotland

Stonehouse was a small hospital and mainly dealt with minor injuries in the Accident and Emergency department, but it was more than just a "cottage hospital". There was an orthopaedic department. I thought this was a good start, giving me a little time to settle, learn, read and prepare for my part one FRCS. Also, this job was recognised for my FRCS training, which was a bonus. My consultant here was Miss S., and she was very pleasant, caring and kind and an excellent orthopaedic surgeon. At Stonehouse hospital the orthopaedic unit was small. Apart from the consultant, there was a registrar and two senior house officers, of which I was one but still the most junior in the team. There was one German doctor, he was permanent and possibly working at an assistant specialist grade. All the junior staff, including the registrar, were Indian.

It was a very interesting bunch. The registrar had already qualified as a surgeon in India and had a post-graduate qualification, known as M.S. — Master of Surgery, in India. He was there to get his FRCS and I imagined wrongly that I had to compete with him for the FRCS because he had for more experience and knowledge. Only twenty percent of students passed, and in truth there was no direct competition like I had in India when I applied for Medical School.

The work wasn't that hard, and everybody got on well. I introduced myself to two of the nursing sisters, Sister T and Sister A. They were both very pleasant and good at their jobs.

I used to work one in two on the rota system for night duty and weekends with the other senior house officer, of course during the day, Monday to Friday we both worked. Working every other night and weekend would now be considered dangerous but back in the day this was normal. No one dared complain, complainers were looked down on as lazy. There was very little social life, so we spent our spare time studying or watching television in the doctors' common room. The only problem with this was that you had to watch what was on because as a new doctor you would not dare change the channel. This is the downside with being a junior member of the team. The only time you got choice was when you were alone. The canteen meals being very cheap and the accommodation being free, I hardly spent a penny, except for educational books for part one of the FRCS. I bought two main books, *Grey's Anatomy* and *Shamson's Physiology*, these were essential reading.

Occasionally we were invited to our registrar's house for a proper home cooked Indian meal. He lived close by with his wife and children. He was a real gentleman and had originally come from Bihar in India. That was our treat, otherwise it was canteen meals. Coming from a country where spice and vibrancy flavoured every meal, the Scottish canteen fare felt very bland to my palate. Then I only used to eat chicken, if that was not on the menu, I used to eat bread and vegetables and that was fine for me. I had been in Scotland a few months and the weather was getting decidedly cooler. This was a totally new experience for me, where I came from, seventy degrees Fahrenheit seemed freezing. One night, when I was on duty, and I got a call from the accident and emergency to see a patient. I think it was around midnight, there was a full moon and a very clear sky. I walked across from my accommodation, looking up at the moon, singing to myself and the next thing I knew, I was flat on my back, as both feet slipped, and I fell!

I could not understand what had happened, I got up, cleaned myself and went to see the patient. Sister T noticed the dirty marks on my white coat. After I finished examining and treating the patient, she asked me what had happened to my coat? I told her both my feet just slipped and I fell and that I didn't understand why.

She just laughed at my innocence and said, 'You daft bugger! Haven't you heard of black ice?'

Of course, my answer was no. The only ice I had ever come into contact with was floating in a drink! I had never seen black ice in my life, this was a new experience for me, and Sister T explained to me in a caring manner how to be careful walking on ice.

Time was going fast and now I had to think about future jobs. I wanted to apply for surgery, although, in hindsight, I would have been better staying there another six months, to get more experience but I was very impatient and wanted to move on fast with my career. The big problem with this was general surgery was the most popular speciality and there was more competition for those jobs and naturally the local graduates, British graduates, had more chance than the overseas graduates, especially in those days.

Overseas graduates mostly got jobs in less popular specialities, like elderly medicine, accident and emergency and psychiatry etc., and this was generally in rural and small district hospitals. I did not realise this at the time, but like many other things I figured it out as time went by and remained determined to try and get into surgery. I found my friend, the

British Medical Journal, in the library and applied for as many jobs as I could all over the country. Obviously, I did not know how to type, there were no computers back then. Instead, I always got someone to help me type my applications. I applied mostly for junior jobs, as a junior house officer, although at the time I was a senior house officer in accident and emergency department. Logically, I thought I had more of a chance of getting a more junior house officer post which worked out well. I got interview for a house officer job at Merthyr Tydfil Hospital in South Wales. I had to ask for time off work to attend the interview and arranged another doctor to cover me. I travelled overnight by a train to Cardiff and then another train to Merthyr Tydfil. My interview went well, and they said they had more candidates and would let me know within a week. After a few days I got a letter to tell me I got the job and I was pleased at how easily I had got the job, it was another step to getting my surgical experience. When the time came to leave my first job and new friends at Stonehouse hospital in the UK, I became quite emotional because it was the beginning of my long road to my future. My consultant, Miss S, both nursing sisters and my registrar were very helpful in this embryonic stage of my surgical life, and they played major part in my development and became part of my future and who I am today. I thanked them all profusely and left a little gift and I was on my way to South Wales.

1974 Merthyr Tydfil

I arrived at Merthyr Tydfil hospital and was met by the admin staff. First, they showed me to my accommodation, which was one room with a bedside table, a lamp and a telephone extension from the switchboard. In those days, you had to go through a switchboard for any calls you made, there were no mobile phones, and we had a thing called a bleep. When it buzzed you had to find the nearest extension and call the switchboard. There was a wash basin and toilet in the room, but I had to share a shower with the other doctors. I was quite happy with it, this hospital was small but there were three general surgeons which meant a larger number of patients than at Stonehouse.

What I liked most about this hospital was that they were all very friendly. I have generally found all the hospitals around the country had friendly environments, but this was something different. I felt I was being treated like one of them. Merthyr Tydfil is a mining town and maybe that created a special community spirit, I don't know, but they were different to a certain extent. My consultant was a Welshman, Mr D.T, he was tall, well-built and like a father figure, a family man. He spoke very softly in a Welsh accent, and I never saw him lose his temper towards anyone at any time. I felt comfortable with him, and I liked him, and I knew I could approach him anytime without fear. I had respect for him, is the right way to put it.

Our team was made up of a consultant, registrar, senior house officer and a junior house officer. There were two other consultants, but my main job was in Mr D. T's unit. The only time I would work for the other consultants was when I was on-call at night or the weekend to cover their patients. The rota again was one night in two and alternate weekends. It was reasonably busy. My work was to admit patients from waiting lists for operations and emergencies admission. I had to take bloods and do all the routine stuff, the sister used to remind me if I had forgotten anything. I followed that rule to always get on with the sisters and nursing staff. I used to go to theatre whenever I could and assist, mostly the registrar and sometimes the consultant. I was getting into a good routine, I used to go to the ward and mark the operation site the night before. This is done to let the surgeon know which site the operation would be, although, they usually checked the notes, this was double security, but for me I had to get it right. That is why I would double check the notes and ask the patient. One time, the other house officer went off sick and they could not get a locum to cover for him, therefore for two weeks I could not leave the hospital. I did get a reasonable amount of sleep at night as it was not that busy, although occasionally, I lost a night's sleep. I learned a lot and got more experience than I would have otherwise. In those days we did not get any extra money for doing extra shifts. That is how it worked but I did not mind because my main aim was to qualify as a surgeon, and I never thought about the money.

My registrar was Indian from Andhra Pradesh, which is in South India bordering with my state of Maharashtra. He had married a British nurse and settled in the UK. I always remember he had very good polite manners. The food at the hospital was from the canteen and as usual it was subsidised. Most of the doctors were from Bihar which is a north-eastern state of India. Although, we were all from India, our dialects and personalities were all different. I had never seen more than two states in India. One being my home state, Maharashtra and the other Gujarat, which is north west of Mumbai, and the state in which the great Mahatma Gandhi was born at a place called Porbandar on the 2nd of October 1869.

My time at Merthyr Tydfil hospital passed quickly and again I had to start looking for another job and continue my nomadic life. Again, I started looking in the British Medical Journal, but surgical senior house officer posts were difficult to apply for as many only wanted doctors who had already passed part one of the FRCS examination or had a lot more experience. This was 'Catch 22', I did not have a lot of surgical experience. I therefore decided to apply for the less popular speciality of neurosurgery, so that I could get a job and some more experience. I applied and got an interview in London at Guy's King's College and Maudsley hospital. I was surprised to even get an interview in the best neurosurgical unit in the country at the time. In fact, all my friends and my consultant were very surprised too, they thought it could be a mistake from their reactions.

I thought there was nothing wrong with going to the interview as it would give me some interview experience. I went and with utmost honesty told them that I had no experience in neurosurgery and that my knowledge was all from text books. To my surprise they offered me the job and I would be given training. This turned out to be the biggest mistake I have ever made in the whole time I have worked in the UK.

To this day my memories are very strong, the whole experience could have ended my dream of becoming a surgeon and possibly my career. I accepted the job with some apprehension, but I thought the consultant, who was the most senior, was a man with excellent manners and very pleasant, and I would be okay.

The truth of the matter was that he had been the one who interviewed me, but I was not going to be working with him, I was going to be working with another consultant and I didn't know anything about this. In any case, I would not have known anything about him, I accepted the job and went back to Merthyr Tydfil.

My post at Merthyr Tydfil was coming towards its end and it was time to say goodbyes. My friend Dr K, I used to call him K'Saab, and he used to call me Jadhavji, I think that's how all the doctors I had known from Bihar used to call each other, not by first name, but with 'ji' attached to your surname.

Dr K decided we should organise a leaving party and invite most of the junior doctors and my consultant Mr D.T. who happily agreed to come along with his wife. I was really pleased about this because he was a gentleman and you could not find a better person, and I was the most junior member of the team, but he treated me well.

Dr K and I arranged all the shopping for that weekend, with plenty of drinks, of course! Dr K was actually quite a good cook, he was a few years senior to me and used to cook for himself regularly, instead of the canteen food.

Between the two of us, me being the assistant and him being the chef, we managed quite a number of Indian dishes, including chicken and lamb. We really had a great time that evening and just as well because my next six months were worst of my time in England.

I packed my suitcase and hand luggage and said thank you to my consultant, registrar and all my doctor friends. I gave a special thanks to the nursing sister and staff and I left a small gift in appreciation.

As I said before, doctors, nurses and all the staff including catering staff treated me like one of their own and it was very emotional for me to leave this place. They had become part of the journey and that will always remain with me.

1974 — London, England

I arrived at Guy's King's college and Maudsley hospital. I had to find my way around Maudsley hospital where my accommodation was. I was shown to my room by admin staff. It's difficult to describe the brusque way he was with me. He was professional but I felt like something was different here compared to the previous hospital experiences. There was no human touch for me as an individual, it was a job; that was it. My accommodation was one room with a bathroom and a bed. I had to use the common kitchen for tea and toast or anything like that. The Guy's King's College and Maudsley hospital was a big complex and one of the best neurosurgical and neurology units in the country at the time. They used to get referrals from all over the UK for specialist treatment, it was a centre of excellence.

Looking back, years later, now it seems very basic. The only invasive investigation was internal carotid angiography, and this was done by a specialist called Dr S who injected dye into the patients' carotid arteries, which are located one on each side of the neck. The carotid arteries provide part of the blood supply to the brain and others were basilar arteries at the back of the neck. The dye outlines all the blood vessels in most parts of the brain supplied by the internal carotid arteries. Then you can compare those to normal ones and make a diagnosis. These are the same arteries we scan these days if someone has had a stroke or a transient ischaemic attack, sometimes called a mild stroke or pre-stroke. This is to find out what the issue is and if there is a blockage in the artery this can be treated with surgery, depending on the severity. This would otherwise be treated with cholesterol lowering drugs, usually statins.

Nowadays, we have an ultrasound, computer tomography

(CT) and magnetic resonance imaging (MRI) scans. With these tools available we do not need to do a carotid angiography any more.

We had two consultants. The more senior one of the two was a gentleman. One of the things I learned from him was that you can be an excellent surgeon without being rude and arrogant. If you were assisting him during an operation he always used to say, excuse me, can you do it this way or that way and never raised his voice. He was a brilliant surgeon, an authority in neurosurgery and had written books.

Then there was a more junior consultant, who was the polar opposite. He was a mediocre surgeon and very rude, not just to me but to a number of the other staff too. Sadly, I was the one who mainly worked with him. I was told in the interview I would be given training but there was none, you had to learn as you went along. I found this very difficult because it was a completely new speciality for me. I only had theoretical knowledge and theory and practical ability are two very different things.

To start, the medical history taking, and examination were very extensive. It could take an hour for one patient. Neurological examination was another problem. For example, when you are assessing reflexes, power, tone and sensation, sometimes it can be very tricky, people are not machines! If you tap, say, below the knee cap, the patella, we are supposed to assess whether it is normal or abnormal. If the knee jerks it's normal, and if it doesn't move at all it is abnormal. If it jerks violently then it's hyperactive. There is a catch though, sometimes you could not tell whether it is hyperactive or normal, especially when you have very little practical experience. This is just an example, it was the same with the

70

muscle power we had to put in one to five grades, and you could get this wrong as well. This is something you learn by experience over a period of time, but this is becoming less and less important now because we have more investigations. The reason I am describing this is because the junior consultant I was working with was well known for his temper towards staff. On one occasion, I had the misfortune of getting properly told off.

Before theatre, I had to put a urinary catheter into this particular patient's bladder. When you put a catheter in, urine comes out and you know the catheter is in the bladder. Then you put 5-10ml of water into the side attachment to fill a small balloon to hold the catheter in the bladder. I thought I had done everything right, but when they were anaesthetising the patient, the catheter came out. This consultant was furious. I was on the ward seeing a patient and a sister hurried up to me, I could tell by her body language it wasn't good news! She said I needed to go to theatre and the consultant wanted to see me immediately. I knew I was in trouble but wasn't sure why? I walked into theatre, and as soon as he saw me, he started screaming and thumping his feet, I thought he was going to have a seizure. His face was red, I was speechless. He said that I had not put enough water in the balloon, this is a big disaster for him! In truth I had put more than enough as far as I recall. Nobody else showed any emotions, as they were all used to it. The worst thing he did, apart from the shouting, was that he said I would never pass the FRCS and become a surgeon. I felt like walking out but for some reason or another, I stayed, finished the job and then walked out. I was left very, very angry and kept asking myself questions, like why I am doing this job, this catheter thing was not a big mistake. All I had to do was put the catheter back in and put a little more water in the balloon, which I did. It was possible whilst trying to put a patient to sleep someone accidentally tugged on the catheter and it came out, which was a possibility but for this consultant, it was a grave mistake. The sad thing was that when his tantrum was over, you would not recognise him as the same person, he would smile at you as if nothing had happened. Once I remember, one junior nurse just walked out from him, when he started shouting at her. I had never been treated like this by anyone, I could not sleep that night. I lay awake thinking about leaving the job and going back to India, but then I thought that would be a failure! I was also thinking about the man, who used to bulk buy from our farm who had told my father that I will be FRCS. How could he be wrong? He did not know what FRCS meant and he probably did not even know where England was! He had no education, not even primary school so his knowledge about it was almost nil.

I decided to ring my good friend, Dr G, in India. We had been good friends since the beginning of medical college days when he used to camp on my hostel floor. I told him what had happened, he listened calmly and then said how long you have you been working there? I said three months. He said, so you only have three more months to go. I said yes. He asked another question, saying that have you got any holidays to take, I said two weeks, then he said, so you have only got ten weeks left to work and during that time, on the weekends, you don't have to see him.

He said, 'Please do not give up, continue there, I have full confidence you will become a FRCS and you will become a successful surgeon, probably better than that surgeon. Remember your namesake, Shivaji. He was a fighter king, he fought the Mughals with only a small army and won.'

I thought that was good advice and it boosted my confidence. I continued and surprisingly, I spent a lot of the rest of my time there working for the senior consultant and had no further tantrums from that junior consultant. My only regret is that I just found the place not as friendly. I was used to the warm, almost family feeling of the previous hospitals, but I gained valuable experience. I managed to learn how to make Burr holes in the skull to remove blood clots from the outer areas of the brain. A Burr hole is when you make a hole in the skull manually, if you suspect blood is pressing on the brain. Another thing I learned was how to do a full and thorough neurological examination and that has helped me throughout my working life, especially as a general practitioner later in my career.

I remember one lady who was referred from a district hospital some way from London. Her medical history was strange. She was getting very angry, agitated and moody and her family took her to the GP, who after history and examination, thought she had depression because her Catholic son was marrying a Protestant girl, which she disapproved of. So, the GP thought it could have caused stress and depression. One day, while she was walking, she fell and banged her head. She was taken to Accident and Emergency and had an X-ray. It was reported as showing an increase in vascularity of the membranes surrounding the brain. This is one of the signs of a meningioma, a tumour of the membranes of the brain. These are more common in women, and usually benign but can cause symptoms when pressing on the brain. She was referred to London with X-rays. She was given an internal carotid angiogram, which showed the meningioma, and all her symptoms were due to the pressure on her brain.

Our senior consultant operated to remove the tumour, it was so large and had caused so much pressure on the brain, which is normally convex outwards had become concave, that was the best way to describe it. I think the tumour was over one pound in weight. This was towards the end of my contract at the hospital. She was still unconscious when I left. I never found out if she recovered or how she progressed. I do know her case made a lasting impression on me, and I always remembered how easy it was to ascribe personality changes to mental health rather than physical health. One of the lasting memories left from the last job at Guy's was the woman who had the meningioma which had been misdiagnosed as stress and depression. It was a very difficult to diagnose, especially in those days.

Finally, I finished this job and said my thank yous to all the staff and a special thank you to my senior consultant. I thanked him for giving me a good reference. I will always be grateful to my senior consultant for this, I kept that with me for years. During my last month I had applied for many jobs. I moved next to Ayr County hospital in Scotland and took up a post in accident and emergency and orthopaedics as a senior house officer.

1974 — Ayr, Scotland

Before I could draw breath, I had moved almost the length of the UK to start my post in Ayr. The A&E department was very busy on Fridays and Saturdays. After a night out people got into fights and many sustained injuries. I was able to manage easily, the nursing staff were excellent at calming these patients. In the orthopaedic part of the job, I was learning about

74

managing fractures and dislocations. At this stage, I was able to reduce quite a few arm fractures, like Colles' wrist fractures. These involve the radius, at the level of the wrist on the thumb side of the bone. This is very common because when you fall, generally onto an outstretched hand and it causes this classic fracture. It's even more common in winter. Usually with the patient either under general anaesthetic or a strong sedative, using a fair amount of pulling you can correct the position of the bone then put the forearm in plaster for four to six weeks. It usually heals well. I think treatment has changed little since I first learnt to reduce Colles fractures.

Although, everything was going okay, I was not really concentrating and enjoying the work as much, whether this was due to the trauma of my previous job, I do not know. Although I am quite resilient, it felt like post-traumatic stress. One evening, I rang my cousin who had just arrived in England and was working in accident and emergency at Stafford general hospital. He suggested that I should go there, because there was going to be a job coming up in a couple months and he would speak to his consultant. He said that I could go whenever I wanted and stay with him, he was staying in a large two-bedroom flat in Standon Hall hospital, which is a very old building. It was a big house converted into an orthopaedic hospital and only planned "cold surgery" orthopaedic operations were carried out there. It was only short distance from Stafford. He did speak to his consultant, who was from India, I think from Bangalore, and he was married to a local girl and was well settled. He advised me to apply for the job, I had some experience working in accident and emergency and I had a good chance.

I took two weeks holiday and two weeks unpaid leave and

left the job from Ayr County to go to Stafford. I had an interview, and all went well, there were two other candidates, but it was fair to say, I did have ten months experience working in accident and emergency and I got the job, I assume it was on merit. One of the advantages of this job was that I now had some social life as well.

1975 — Stafford General Hospital
I was now working as a senior house officer in the accident and emergency department at Stafford General Hospital. This was a medium-sized district hospital and had all the major specialities and also Standon Hall Hospital for planned orthopaedic surgery. The consultants used to travel there once or twice a week. Most of the junior doctors were overseas graduates, most commonly of Indian or Pakistani origin but also there were a few Greek doctors. Our consultant was Mr K, he was Indian and married to local girl. He was calm and had a quiet nature and I felt very comfortable talking to him. Stafford is very near to the M6 motorway and there were many times we saw major accident injuries from the frequent crashes.

One incident which sticks in my mind concerned a young man probably in his twenties who was involved in a horrific motorbike accident. I know doctors are supposed to be "bullet proof" but it upset me to see his injuries. There was a compound (open) fracture of his skull, his brain was visible but worse still, part of the brain was coming through his nose. He did not survive long enough to be transferred to the specialist unit.

I helped treat several variations of chest and abdominal injuries. Our job was to assess and pass on to other specialities

76

for further management, broken teeth went to maxillary-facial, fractures to orthopaedics and internal trauma to general surgery. Neurological issues were 'blue-lighted' to Birmingham. Our consultant Mr K also performed emergency operations when time was of the essence, such as splenectomy for a ruptured spleen. This is time sensitive and if left too long the patient would die of blood loss, swift action was imperative. It was good experience for a trainee surgeon.

Our accommodation was in a new building where doctors were accommodated in flats with a shared kitchen and a common room where we would watch TV in our spare time. There was also a hospital canteen for meals but once the doctors (at least some) got to know each other, we used to cook evening meals on a sort of rota basis. Whichever doctors were on the early shifts used to make the food for all of us. This worked really well, also we enjoyed a social drink. Whiskey was the preference, particularly Johnnie Walker Black Label. It is not commonly known, but Indian men like whiskey. Obviously, some did not, but there was a core number who enjoyed a drink after work.

One evening, I was on a late shift and this particular night did not finish until eight p.m. when the night doctor took over. I came home quite hungry because I had missed my lunch and they were already having drinks. These drinkers were jolly and as soon as I walked in, I was given a half glass of neat whiskey. I got changed and had a drink but as soon as I finished one, someone would pour another half glass of whiskey, I can't remember whether I had two or three. All I can remember, is that I was feeling dizzy and sick, and I managed to get to the bathroom, but before I could reach the sink or the toilet, I was violently sick. After being sick, I managed to get into my bed with the help of my friends and that was it, I didn't wake up until the next morning. Luckily, my duty next day was an afternoon shift and I had recovered enough by then to go to work. I must say I do not remember being sick after drinking again in my life, although I have had excess amounts of alcohol on several occasions! One thing I learnt was not to drink a large amount of whisky on an empty stomach, especially not neat whiskey.

My social life was getting better, and I enjoyed my job and got on well with my consultant and the nurses, very well. I was getting a reasonable wage and felt I could afford a car, so I bought an Opel Manta, 2 litre sports version. It was a very fast car. I had been driving in India and I was allowed to drive with an L plate as long as someone with a full UK driving license was sitting next to me. I used to drive my sports car Indian style, it was difficult to get rid of old habits. The rules were a little different in the UK, but I was younger, and I thought I could do anything. I thought if I just took three or four lessons, I would easily pass my test. I booked some driving lessons and in the meantime our friends said that we should do a UK tour from Stafford to Hull to visit other doctor friends, and then go to Newcastle and travel north to Aberdeen, Edinburgh and back. So, I took a week's holiday and we set off, sharing the driving on the way. My friends said to me, this way I could have a lot of experience. We came back safely, I do not know how but we managed. I took a few lessons, although the instructor did not think I was ready for the test, he booked it anyway. So naturally I failed my test on two accounts; firstly, crossing my hands on the steering wheel and secondly, reversing, I gather I was not quite accurate. That was that, rather a shock to my system and pride. Of course, I took a few more lessons and passed at the second attempt. I was now officially free to drive on my own. I was quite happy and had been studying for my part one of the FRCS and my job seemed to be secure for at least twelve months. During this time, we used to have parties and invite the nurses. On one such occasion, I met a student nurse, she was good looking and petite at only five feet tall. She had a kind heart and always used to smile and laugh. I liked her and I think she liked me too. We started going out initially as casual friends, but we got on well and the friendship developed into a steady relationship as boyfriend and girlfriend.

Finally, I passed part one of the FRCS and that meant I was half way to becoming a Fellow of the Royal College of Surgeons. I was really pleased because I could now apply for surgical jobs though it was still difficult to get a surgical post. The available posts were those where you had to go into a rotation with other specialities, like orthopaedics and accident and emergency. I have no problem with orthopaedics or accident and emergency as I had enough experience already, but I really needed surgery to progress further, and it was one of the requirements to sit for the final FRCS examination.

I asked my consultant for his advice, and he suggested I try and get a rotation because that way I have more of a chance of further surgical jobs, but he also said if I wanted to continue at Stafford, he would extend my contract but in my best interest he said try to get another job, how right he was.

I put in a number of applications all over the United Kingdom and I got an interview at War Memorial Hospital, Wrexham, which combined with Maelor General Hospital. I got offered a post as a senior house officer with an eighteen-month contract. This was the longest stay at one hospital after

Stafford. I did six months in accident and emergency, six months in orthopaedic and both of these jobs were based at War Memorial Hospital and the last six months were at Maelor General Hospital, in North Wales.

My only problem was that I had my girlfriend to consider, she was a newly qualified staff nurse in Stafford, she couldn't just move. We really got on well, I do not remember ever having an argument, but despite this relationship my career had to progress. She understood and we still kept seeing each other regularly at weekends and sometimes during the week. I finished my time at Stafford and thanked my consultant for his guidance and the nursing staff and all the doctors. I left some presents for the consultants and staff, said my goodbyes, and left with a heavy heart. I enjoyed everything at Stafford and took with me some really happy memories and invaluable hands-on experience.

1976 War Memorial Hospital, Wrexham — Accident and Emergency

The first part of the rotation was as a senior house officer in Accident and Emergency department. This was the usual routine SHO work, I already had lot of experience in A and E, it was not that difficult of a job. I think I was overqualified for this position in a way, but still enjoyed what I did. I was still seeing my girlfriend whenever we could. She used to ring me almost every night and all the calls came through the switchboard. The switchboard was very quiet at night, and I often wondered if the switchboard staff listened to our conversations but whenever she used to put through the call, the switchboard operator used to laugh and say, 'Guess who it is? It's little me!' She always used to start a conversation with,

"It's little me". One of the sweetest things she did was send me printed love letters from a booklet she had. She must have bought it, for every single day of the month. The only problem with our relationship was that she was looking for something permanent and to settle down and have a family. Sadly, my situation being what it was, this wasn't something I could foresee at the time. Even though I had passed the part one FRCS examination, I did not have a permanent job. I did not know what I was going to do. I still thought I would return to India when I became a surgeon. She was very unsettled with my nomadic lifestyle, and it was very hard for both of us. I got on well with all her family and always felt accepted.

1976 — War Memorial Hospital Wrexham — Orthopaedic

The War Memorial Hospital changed its name in 1986, but this was the name whilst I was there. My next six months was in the orthopaedic department which had two consultants, Mr H and Mr J. I was attached to Mr J's team as a senior house officer. He was an excellent orthopaedic surgeon. So was Mr H although I hardly worked with him, except for when his senior house officer was on holiday. The War Memorial hospital, orthopaedic unit was linked to the Agnes Hunt hospital. The full title for this hospital was the Robert Jones and Agnes Hunt hospital. The hospital was originally established in Baschurch by Miss Agnes Hunt as the Baschurch children's hospital in 1900. Agnes Hunt consulted Sir Robert Jones, after whom the hospital was also named. She wanted his opinion on her own illness in 1903 and he became the honorary surgeon to the hospital in 1904. The hospital moved to the present site in Oswestry in Shropshire as the Shropshire Orthopaedic hospital in 1921 and then became the

Robert Jones and Agnes Hunt hospital in 1933. During the Second World War the hospital took badly injured patients under the Ministry of Health's Emergency Services Act, this was before the NHS. John Charnley, the leading orthopaedic surgeon, worked in the hospital for six months in 1946. Later, it joined the National Health Service in 1948. We had to go to lectures and meetings there at least once a month. My professor at Aurangabad Medical college had done part of his training here, it was a small link to my motherland.

Gradually, the relationship with my girlfriend became too difficult to continue, we both decided to part on amicable terms. Although sad, it was best that we loosened the bonds and we kept in contact for a while. I think she eventually became a midwife and got married. Maybe it was Fate, someone else was there for me?

1977 — Maelor general hospital, Wrexham

Finally, I moved to Maelor General Hospital, where I took up my post as senior house officer in surgery with a consultant called, Mr T. Like an army officer, you could hear his footsteps from one end of the corridor to the other. Other doctors had warned me that he was very difficult to work with, but I just followed his instructions and his way of working and things went smoothly. He had his own set of surgical instruments made especially for him. I had no problems with that, it worked for him, he was a good surgeon. He liked everything to be neat and tidy on the ward and everybody was used to it. I am naturally very punctual, and I used to go to the ward at eight a.m. every morning to make sure everything was ready. I think I got on well with him and, in fact, he let me do an appendicectomy and other minor operations. I guess, what he liked about me was that I was hard-working and never avoided extra work. I also followed his routine without questioning him.

There was another surgeon who I will call Mr T.O. It was very difficult to get on his unit because he was an examiner for the part two of the FRCS in London. It was natural that doctors wanted to work with him. I saw him in meetings sometimes and also in teaching sessions. He was a pleasant and likeable man. I got a feeling there was not much friendship between Mr T.O. and Mr T, of course, this was my personal opinion.

One of the best things about North Wales was the really beautiful countryside just a short drive away. I remember my orthopaedic registrar Mr J and a few others going for drinks in the country pubs. I used to drive more often than not. One of the things I liked was chicken and chips in the basket in a rustic Welsh country pub, set in the glorious surroundings. Everybody knows how beautiful Snowdonia is, but my favourite place was Dolgellau. Sometimes I used to drive there with other doctor friends or one or two nurses and occasionally on my own as soon as I had finished for the day. I would spend the evening just walking around as I have always liked natural beauty, whether in the forest, the lakes or the seaside, as long as there were plenty of palm trees! Of course, not in North Wales. I found a marked difference between South and North Wales. I think North Wales was richer, but I liked both very much. I am happy that I worked in both parts of Wales.

Now my time was coming to move on as my eighteen-month contract was almost up. Again, I had to apply for new jobs and this time I had a better opportunity to apply for a surgical post, rather than a rotation. I had a lot more experience and in passing my part one of the FRCS examination, it indicated I was seriously interested in becoming a surgeon. I knew it was not going to be easy because it was one of the most popular specialties. Of course, local graduates had a better chance than me, but I did not want to give up. I applied for many jobs, I lost count, anywhere and everywhere in the country, except London!

Finally, I received an invitation for an interview at Blackburn Royal Infirmary in Lancashire. I went early and visited the surgical wards and introduced myself to the surgical sisters as well as the theatre staff, I made every effort to show interest. Finally, I had the interview and did well, I answered all the questions correctly, in my view. There were four other candidates for the one job, but it was a good thing none of them were local graduates, as far as I knew. Finally, I was called in and told that I had got the job and that it was for twelve months. I was also told that it could be extended a further six months. I was over the moon because I knew that there was a fair chance I would be able to pass the FRCS, and who knows, maybe get a registrar position here. Some people might think I was dreaming too high. I still think fate decides your future.

I went back to Wrexham and stayed there until the end of my contract. I was more relaxed knowing that I had a job to go to and that it was in general surgery. When it was time to leave, I said my usual thanks to my consultant Mr T and the nursing staff. I was pleasantly surprised that Mr T had written an excellent reference for me. I packed my good old friend, my suitcase, and put it in the car and I was off to my new destination.

Towards the end of my contract at Wrexham I met a Scottish doctor, ED. We used to sit in the doctor's sitting room and watch TV together. Over time we started chatting and became friends. She was slim with short, dark curly hair and blue eyes. She had a gentle manner and we got on well. We went out for drinks a few times, the TV was not much good back in the day and talking to her was far more interesting, but I finished my job and was moving to Blackburn. Before I left, we promised to see each other again. I gave her my new address and hospital telephone number, in those days there were no mobile phones.

1978 — Blackburn Royal Infirmary, Lancashire

I arrived in Blackburn and was shown to my accommodation by the friendly admin staff. I settled easily into Blackburn Royal Infirmary life. My accommodation was in an old house, probably an old mill owner's mansion. It was situated across the road from the Royal Infirmary and had been converted into doctors' accommodation. I had a bedroom with the one bed side table and a small drawer, a shower, a toilet and a wash basin, a kitchen and a tea/coffee making facilities where in the common kitchen for all the junior doctors. I was happy with that arrangement, because lunch was in the hospital canteen for all the doctors. Sometimes I cooked, otherwise, I used to go out to a pub or restaurant. I had accumulated a selection of spices on my travels. I kept them tucked away in a carrier bag. Fresh meat was difficult to source, shops did not stay open and when you are on-call it was impossible to go supermarket shopping. In the doctors' accommodation there was only one communal fridge and food either "walked" or crawled away, forgotten and rancid! Cleverer men than me had found the perfect solution to this problem in the form of KFC. If you wanted to make a curry, buy a 5-piece dinner and use the chicken for a curry! It was pure genius. The spices in the KFC crumb coating blended perfectly with my array of spices, I could produce a quick tasty dinner without risking food poisoning or theft!

The surgical unit in Blackburn was overseen by four general surgeons and one urologist. It was a reasonably busy unit, I thought I would get surgical experience here, working with all four general surgeons, you are going to learn different skills, ways and decision-making. It was really good in a way to learn fast.

Blackburn was a typical old northern mill town, and by the late 1970s had become a multi-racial population with various nationalities. There were Polish and Italian communities dating back to the Second World War. Generally, overseas workers were originally brought over from India and Pakistan to work in the mills. Eventually men brought their wives, specialist food shops, clothes shops and food businesses began to spring up. There are still quite a number of old buildings and mills, but Blackburn has seen many changes over the decades after the Second World War. One advantage of moving into town like this was that we could get Indian spices very easily and also go out to eat in Indian restaurants. Restaurant food may not be like we'd eat at home, it had been altered to cater for the British palate, but it was a welcome addition. I was getting used to life in and outside of the hospital. At the time I was single and had no attachments and I used to go with other single doctors, I have been known to frequent the Cat's Whiskers in Burnley and go gambling in the Playboy club in Manchester. Sometimes married Indian doctors used to join us without telling their wives, but it was good fun.

We began going to nightclubs around Blackburn, Burnley

and Preston. Occasionally, we went to Manchester as well, so we had an exciting bachelor's social life but while we played hard, we worked hard as well, but I always made time for my old friends and my cousins.

I was still in contact with ED, we spoke on the phone occasionally. One day she rang and asked me how my new job was going, after a short chat I asked her if she would like to come and see me at the weekend? She said yes, she would love to. We arranged to find a free weekend and she came up on the Friday by train. I picked her up from the station, she stayed with me in my accommodation. On the Saturday we went to the Yorkshire Dales and had a walk and enjoyed the countryside. That evening I took her out for a meal in a local restaurant, we had a very enjoyable time. On the Sunday we drove through the Trough of Bowland, it's a scenic area and we stopped by the River Hodder and walked on the river bank and had a picnic. That evening I dropped her at the station and said goodbye. Soon after she finished her contract at Wrexham and moved onto another job. She did give me her new address but somehow, we lost touch and I never saw her again. I sometimes wonder what happened to her in life. I always remember her as a good friend in my life's journey. By now I was studying hard for my part two FRCS, I still planned to get my Fellowship then return to India.

I can remember one of our parties at the doctor's residence, the nurses were invited, and I happened to meet a student nurse who seemed interested in me. After that she kept appearing wherever I was and after a couple more encounters on the ward I asked her out for a drink. We started going out regularly and became an item. We even took a holiday to St Lucia, where I had my first taste of the Caribbean and a "proper" holiday. I had saved up and bought my first house in Clayton le Moors, it was a three-bedroom semi-detached house, my girlfriend helped me decorate. Initially everything was going well, again, I got on with her parents and was always made to feel very welcome in their home, but as time went by the shine began to tarnish on our relationship. We argued and bickered frequently. We were not compatible, eventually, we split up, it was a mutual agreement, and we went our separate ways. This was quite emotional, but I felt it was best for both of us.

Around this time, I passed part two of the FRCS examination. This was before we split up, and she came to my degree receiving ceremony in Scotland with me.

So, now I was a Fellow of Royal College of Surgeons, I had accomplished what I came for. It felt good but at the same time I knew this was where the real practical training in surgery began. At first, I worked under supervision but later on I would have to take on operating on my own and have my own operating list.

Although I had passed my examination, I had my own house, a new car and plenty of friends around, for whatever reason I felt a bit unsettled. I think the break-up wasn't as simple as I thought. We still worked in the same hospital and now she was a staff nurse on the surgical wards sometimes it could be a little difficult. I needed a change of scenery and decided to take a two-week holiday, travelling on my own. I bought a return plane ticket and booked my first night's accommodation from the travel agent in Accrington and went to California.

Just before I decided to go to America, I got friendly with one of the nurses I worked with. She had recently finished with a long-term boyfriend and was quite upset about it. As I had recently split with my girlfriend we started talking and became quite good friends. We saw each other a few times for drinks, when I mentioned I was booking a holiday in California she said she could join me for the trip. I thought quite hard about it. I knew we got on well but emotionally I was not sure about my future and wanted time to myself to think about my future. I did not want to stay in the UK, neither did I want to go back to India. In India I could easily find work in a government hospital or start a private practice but not everyone can afford private medical care and it would be difficult for me to ask people for money they didn't have. Anyway, I told her I would have loved her to come with me, but I needed time to myself to think about my future, she seemed fine about it. Looking back, I don't know what would have happened if she had come with me, I will never know. I believe in fate. We remained on friendly terms. Eventually she married a colleague of mine and they have been happy together. My future was with someone else, is all I can think of.

My flight was from London to Los Angeles. I arrived and went through customs and there was no problem although I had an Indian passport. However, when I walked out of customs, a tall American guy started following me and asking me questions. He was friendly enough and seemed to be just asking the sort of things travellers meeting at airports asked each other, like why I was travelling alone, where was I staying but then he began asking what I thought of the Indian Prime Minister, Indira Gandhi?

Indira Gandhi was known to have good relations with Russia in the late 1970s. My answers were honest. I told him I was a doctor working in the UK and had just passed my fellowship and before I continued my surgical training I decided to come on holiday. I told him I was alone because I had recently split from my girlfriend. As for Indira Gandhi, I did not know much about her, because I left India five years ago. It may be just a coincidence, but it was strange, the only thing I can think of is that I used to write letters to my friends in India and complain about the unfairness of capitalism based on what little knowledge I had, but later on I have learned not to believe everything you read or watch on TV. Anyway, I had no further problems as I walked to a taxi, and he left. He did not have any bags with him which most travellers do, I got in a taxi and went to the Holiday Inn hotel. I was very tired but could not get to sleep. There was a fridge in my room with plenty of alcoholic drinks. I think I had a few vodka and tonics and wrote in the book to declare I had used them. I fell asleep and didn't wake until after breakfast time. I had not really planned anything like what to see or do so I thought I would hire a car and tour the city. Well, that didn't go down well! I was still jet-lagged, and I'd never driven on the right side of the road before. In those days there was no SatNav. I had to look at a tourist map and the road signs and drive. You get the picture how this is going to end up? After a couple miles and a few horns blowing at me, I decided to give up the brilliant idea of driving and took the car back. I explained the problem and they were very good with me, they just took the car back and did not charge me anything. I was very impressed. After I got married and had a family, I have driven coast to coast in the state of Florida many times. My family's favourite destination is Disneyland, Florida and we have been about eleven times. I am not sure that's a record, but I was very happy for the whole family.

After the car fiasco I went back to the Los Angeles Holiday Inn and asked at the reception about any attractions they could recommend, of course they were only too pleased to help. They told me about a tour around Hollywood and Beverly Hills and suggested if I wanted the sunset cruise, they could arrange that for me. I duly booked the Hollywood and Beverley Hills tour. I travelled on the tour bus with a guide, explaining about Hollywood and the movies. They drove us through to see the palatial mansions of various film stars and the Hollywood elite. It was interesting but I cannot say it's the type of thing for me, but I can say that I have seen it. Then I booked to go to the island of Santa Catalina by boat, so I could see the island and enjoy the sunset cruise. Santa Catalina is in the Pacific Ocean and it's one of the Channel Islands which lie south-west of Los Angeles. Its highest point is Mount Orizaba at about 2097 feet. I stayed in a hotel for two nights and went on the sunset cruise and took a trip. The mountain island is about twenty miles long and eight miles wide. I really enjoyed seeing this beautiful place, it was so different from anything I had previously seen and then I finished the trip with the spectacular sunset cruise. Then it was back to the Holiday Inn and further planning. I decided to go to Las Vegas and booked a coach, I reached there in the evening, had a meal and spent all night going to different casinos and watching everything, it was so spectacular. There were so many different games and slot machines. I must've lost a few dollars, but it was an experience and well worth it. I had a couple more days left and so I decided to spend a day at Disney. I went by public transport so that I could see more of Los Angeles. I enjoyed my day at Disney, going on the big rides. I liked the fast rollercoaster type of rides. How life changes as with my subsequent visits to Florida Disney, I was not that bothered about fast rides, but I had to go because the children still enjoyed it. That was the end of my stay at Los Angeles, the two weeks passed quite quickly, but I did see quite a lot. I was more relaxed and ready to go back to work again.

When I arrived back at Blackburn Royal Infirmary, I found out there was a registrar post becoming available and it was already advertised in the British Medical Journal. By now, I had eighteen months of surgical experience and performed many routine surgical procedures, like varicose veins and hydrocele drainage which involved draining fluid from around the testicles. My repertoire was growing. All the consultants, nursing sisters and the operating theatre staff were happy with me. I used to go out socially for drinks with the theatre staff and porters, that's what they were called back then, but now it has changed to operating department assistant.

I spoke to the consultants I was working with, and they suggested I apply for the registrars post now I had passed my FRCS, I had as good a chance as anybody else. I think that was good enough for me, although, they did not promise me anything. At the interview, there were four other candidates, and my interview went well. There were three consultants interviewing, the two Mr Bs and Mr M. They asked me the usual surgical and personal questions. One of them was if I am called out in at night for an emergency surgery how would I deal with it, my answer was that I will do it if it was straightforward but if there was any doubt I will ask for advice and help. They were satisfied with that, and they were trying to find out if I was safe. I think as a surgeon, patient safety is paramount and on occasion some doctors, once they had passed the FRCS, become over confident. That is what I have observed during my career. I got the job, and my contract was for eighteen months, the first six months at Accrington Victoria Hospital and the rest at Blackburn Royal Infirmary. This was very good for me because it was reasonably quiet and had very few emergencies. How things fall into place. All the consultants had out-patient and operation lists. and there was one registrar, that's me, one senior house officer and two junior house officers. The nursing staff were really friendly and good at their jobs. As a unit, Accrington worked very well, and it also gave me ample opportunity to do elective surgery. This means all the patients who were on waiting lists for procedures such as cholecystectomy — removal of the gall bladder, repair of hernias, stripping of varicose veins, bowel surgery and many more procedures but no urology operations. These were only carried out at Royal Blackburn Hospital, where I would spend the last twelve months of my contract.

During this period, I used to stay at my house. I went there on days off and weekends, I could relax more and grow some vegetables. There was an added advantage with this place, there was a large playing field called Wilson's playing field near-by and it had a proper running track. In those days, one of my hobbies was running and sometimes badminton. I did not know what my future plans were, but I had the house even though I might not stay in the United Kingdom, I thought that I could always sell it. I did manage to grow some vegetables and I gave some to my neighbours. I think it was cauliflower and beans, it gave me a sense of achievement. I used to play badminton with the nurses and doctors at Hyndburn Sports Centre, then later on when I was working at Blackburn, at Shadsworth Sport Centre. I was quite happy with my social life. I really began to love the British culture and social life, especially Christmas parties. The sadness of my past relationship faded but I was still single and enjoying my life. I began to make more UK friends. I still had my motherland friends and my cousins who were also working towards their FRCS. I began to go out with the local junior doctors when I worked with at Accrington. I have such happy memories.

One in particular, used to take me on adventures. He was a junior house officer, with a wicked sense of humour, I found him very funny, and he used to make me laugh. On our lunch breaks we used to go for a pub lunch together. Life was more relaxed in the late 1970s, we got up to things we couldn't get away with now. Consultants smoked pipes and junior doctors came back to work after lunch with a cheerful smile! This particular friend was married to a nurse, later on I got to know his family as well. We used to drive up to the Lake District sometimes when we were off duty. He was an excellent doctor to have as your colleague, he was quick and sharp with work. He was planning to become a general practitioner, therefore, after this job he went onto a general practice rotation scheme at Blackburn Royal Infirmary and Queens Park Hospital. I was really sad when he left but he had found his own career path. He used to like fishing and I don't know if that is one of the reasons why he moved to Canada? I believe there are a lot of lakes there and I saw some of his photos where he was fishing in Canada. It's always nice to see their family pictures. I will always remember him as an excellent doctor with a good sense of humour.

Another house officer I worked with was E.B. She was a very thorough, kind and caring doctor. She only used to stay at Victoria Hospital when she was on call. We were really good friends and I remember she invited me to her house for a meal with her husband in Preston. Of course, she has moved on, but I still have some happy memories from working together. We lost contact for a while, but I believe she is working in a hospice. One thing I will never forget was one particular incident, concerning a junior doctor. Now I was at the level of registrar, I also had responsibility for teaching my juniors and they used to assist me during operations. I would spend time explaining everything clearly, what I was doing and why. My approach was by now habit and something I did with all my junior doctor colleagues. One time, I was doing a varicose vein operation, which means I had to tie off the long saphenous vein in the groin, but the one important safety point is you must not tie this vein unless you can clearly identify the junction with the deep vein called the femoral vein in your leg. This is the main vein in your leg, which carries deoxygenated blood from your leg back to your heart, there is one on both sides of your legs. If, by accident, if you tie this vein there will be serious problems with the blood drainage from the leg. The saphenous vein joins this vein in the groin, but it can be removed to deal with varicose veins because you can manage without it. Obviously, I aimed to impress the importance of not tying off the wrong portion of the vein and why it was important to recognise this junction. One day, one of the junior doctors was assisting a senior house officer, I was in the next theatre doing my surgery list. This junior doctor asked the senior house officer who was doing the varicose operation if he could show her the junction of the saphenous vein and femoral vein, to which the senior house officer tried to fob her off. This raised a red flag to my young colleague, and she insisted because she knew it was not right. She then, very bravely asked him to stop and said she was going to ask me to come and check if he was correct because the junior doctor was not happy. So, she hurried into my theatre and explained what was going on and this sent alarm bells ringing for me! I went into the next theatre and asked the SHO to show me the junction. Of course, he could not, and he had the ligature around the femoral vein, which he was going to tie. I took over and dissected it a bit more and exposed the junction clearly, then he could safely tie the superficial long saphenous vein. I was relieved that the patient did not come to any harm, and I was very grateful to the junior doctor for saving the day. I am sure that the senior house officer would never make that mistake again.

Now my job at Accrington Victoria Hospital was coming to an end and I had to go back to Blackburn. I was very sorry to leave Accrington. I had so many happy memories, it was a small, friendly community of doctors, nurses and domestic staff and felt more like family to me, at the time. One thing I missed was my toast and cup of morning tea. Our domestic lady, B, looked after our accommodation. Every morning she was on duty she used to bring me toast and tea, even though I don't think it was in her contract. When I left, I gave her something in appreciation.

I met so many nice people in my journey to become a doctor and a surgeon and I will always remember that in the world I had known, there were more nice, dedicated, and genuine people, than bad people.

After my stint in Accrington, I moved back to Blackburn Royal Infirmary where I was going to do the next six months of my general surgery. The Royal Infirmary was a district general hospital and had a busy surgical unit, with four general surgeons and one urologist. I worked with all of them, at one time or another. I learned something different from their own individual good points. This sounds strange but they all had little ways and habits they had developed during their career. Although, the operation was the same, they all worked slightly differently.

Mr B, was a very pleasant and meticulous man in everything he did, especially skin closure after an operation. He used to use this continuous suture and to look at it, it was beautiful but to take them out was not very easy, but staff were used to it. When I did an operation on his list, I used to do the same continuous suture, but I must say I did not like it, but you just stick to their way of doing things. That was his trademark, as soon as you looked at the wound on a ward walk around, as a registrar you knew who had done the operation. The only problem I found with him was he used to take longer than any other surgeon and I used to lose concentration and I had to be careful not to show him any disrespect.

Then there was Mr M, he was quick at both decision-making and operating, he had a natural skill, and I preferred his way, and I learned a lot from him. He did interrupted sutures which were quick to do and easier to remove but the results were no different. Sadly, both Mr M and Mr B have passed away but in their own way they left their mark on my career and they were part of my journey. I still have a small watercolour picture Mr B painted and gave to me as a gift.

As a man from a faraway land, I am very grateful to them for being a part of my life, whatever you see and learn you develop your own style and ways of doing things. I have to say, in those six months, I learned a lot and did most of the major surgeries, also emergency surgeries. I felt like I had finally become a surgeon but there is always more to learn. There is sometimes a downside to it, like any other jobs.

Especially in my job because we are dealing with the human emotions.

One night, I admitted a six-month-old baby as an emergency with what looked like a strangulated inguinal groin hernia. Nowadays, they would go directly to the paediatric surgical department and not to the general surgical ward. I had performed many strangulated hernia operations and I was confident enough to do it that night. You cannot wait, especially if the bowel is caught in the hernia, it can become gangrenous and burst causing life threatening peritonitis. As a matter of safety and protocol, I rang the on-call consultant. Protocol dictates I inform him in case there was any difficulties and I needed to ask him to come and help me. I had done the operation on slightly older children but not a six months old baby, but the anatomy is the same. The on-call consultant said he could trust me, he had full confidence I could cope but to call him if necessary. When you were doing surgery there are a lot of other people involved, like the anaesthetist, theatre nurse and the theatre porters.

I explained all the complications and why we had to do the operation that night and the mother signed the consent form. All was then done legally so the theatre porter put the diathermy pad under the baby's buttocks and the diathermy electrodes were arranged properly, so that I could use the electrodes to stop the bleeding during the operation. It was quite a standard procedure back then. The operation went according to plan, I released a small loop of small bowel, after freeing it from the hernia. It was viable. There was some inflammation due to the constriction, but it looked a good colour and peristalsis (the natural movement of the intestine) began after the release. In other words, it was going to be okay.

I explained to the mother, and she seemed really grateful. But next morning the nursing staff noticed a small red area identified as a burn on the buttocks, possibly due to the diathermy pad. Again, I explained to the mother that it will need a dressing for a week or so, but he should recover, possibly with a small scar on his buttock. I thought she accepted this as one of the complications. The child did well and had no complications from the surgery and he was discharged within a week and a follow-up appointment was booked, I was pleased with the results. Back then it was normal to keep people in hospital for a week or more, now they would probably be sent home the next day. Two months later, I saw the baby in out-patients and checked everything and he was well except for the small scar over his buttocks. I was sure it would fade further, the mother never said much about it. Three months later, we received a letter of complaint about the scar on his buttocks from her solicitors asking for compensation. At first, I was angry, because how could anybody complain when you saved a baby's life and had a very small scar as a result. I discussed this with my consultant as he had a lot more experience with dealing with this sort of problems than I had. He reassured me, he said, firstly you are not responsible for the diathermy pad, and secondly, it's a small scar and one of the complications. He said pass this on to the defence union, which I did with all the details about the operation, the consent and everything. Absolutely nothing came out of it, and neither she nor the solicitor got anything. This showed the other side of human nature. My consultant told me that if I wanted to be a surgeon, I had better get used to it, because I'm going to see complications irrespective of your best efforts. This didn't stop me being upset but it was a learning curve and that's why we have the defence union to defend us.

Recently, one of our consultants who retired, died and there was an obituary in the local paper. He was very well liked and not only a good doctor, but he was very good to all the staff. There were a lot of staff putting comments on social media, my wife noticed some of the old pictures from Accrington Victoria Hospital where I had some happy memories as a surgical registrar. I remember playing a charity football match that was doctors versus nurses. A professional Blackburn Rovers football player was co-opted to play on the nurses' team. In those days I used to be very fit and could run quite fast. I managed to run and keep up with him to get the ball, being a professional footballer, he did not like me competing with him. He put his elbow in my chest and pushed me hard and I fell over and sustained an injury to my sternum. I got up and kept playing but after the match I started to get pain in my sternal area and subsequently an X-ray showed a crack fracture in my sternum. Obviously, there was not any treatment apart from painkillers. The only disadvantage was I could not put my seatbelt on for quite a while. There was a photo of that period on media site I recognised, and it was my registrar in that photo when I was a senior house officer. I remember quite well, he was pleasant and easy going, but always used to complain every time he did surgery. I used to assist him when he was doing surgery, he always used to say, "this is a difficult operation" every single time and, "the organ is very deep" in a particular voice. Therefore, we used to make a joke about it whenever he started operating, he did not realise why we were laughing and everybody in the theatre knew what it meant except him. Sadly, he died in his sixties from a brain tumour.

I was doing fine on the whole, with the surgeries I was performing, there were good results, and I got the opportunity to do many major procedures. I had my operating list as a registrar and was operating independently and I didn't need help. I was lucky in that respect, my surgical skills were good, quick and efficient and I used to finish work in time. If I was not on-call for an evening I used to ring a friend and go out for a drink. Usually, I used to go out with the theatre porters. I had a lot of respect for them and the nurses and all the staff. I always believed in successful surgery being a team effort. However, some of the consultants did not approve of me mixing as I did, but that did not bother me. It never has ever bothered me since being a child, I always treated everyone equally. In fact, one particular consultant asked me if I went to the pub for a drink and to that I said yes. He seemed quite surprised and said that he only goes to restaurants to eat with his family. One evening, one of the junior doctors, let's call him C, asked me if I wanted to go out for a drink, I happily agreed. He organised a date and time and as I was driving, I picked him up. Then, he said he'd forgotten to mention, he had asked someone else, a charge nurse, to join us if it was okay with me? I said I had no problem with it, I had heard about this charge nurse. In a small hospital you knew most of the staff, especially if you are an outgoing person like me. I picked him up as well, and then they gave directions to where we were going. We went to this pub in Accrington, although I had worked there for a while, I had never heard of it, and as we went in, I was quite surprised there were no ladies, only men! This junior doctor got our drinks and we stood near the bar. Standing here I could have a good look around. I said to him why there were no ladies here? Both looked surprised by my question. I said because I have nothing against men, but I prefer ladies' company and is it possible if we could go somewhere else after this drink. They agreed and we went to another pub and had a drink and then I dropped them back at the hospital. Although I am writing this, I must make absolutely clear I respect all LGBT people, but in this case, it was rather the way it was done. If they had told me beforehand where they were planning to go, I would have been more than happy to go and have drink with them at that pub, no problem at all. In fact, I have very good friends in the LGBT community and frequently meet up in the pub for drinks. I personally, and as a doctor have always tried to treat everybody with respect and dignity. The junior doctor apologised to me next day, he did not have to, it is one of those things and we were still friends.

This was a district hospital and we, as surgeons, did most of the surgical procedures except specialist surgeries like cardiac and pulmonary surgery, and of course neurosurgery but those specialities were still not really well developed like they are today. In general, I had a broad field of experience, thus said, because we often did technically difficult procedures which we rarely could practice, except in emergencies! I had to be very careful and have extra concentration. This meant that the night before specific surgeries, for example if I was to perform a thyroidectomy, I would not go out for a drink and have an early night in.

The thyroid is the gland in the front part of your neck, which I have written about previously. If it becomes enlarged, it can press on the trachea, the windpipe. There were a number of reasons for the development of a swelling, called a goitre, which was the most common cause. Sometimes cancer can cause swelling and require surgery, but an operation like this used to scare me. I used to worry about the complications, for example damaging the recurrent laryngeal nerve. The recurrent laryngeal nerve is a branch of vagus nerve coming from the brain. This nerve supplies what we call intrinsic muscles of the larynx, which are responsible for the voice, and it lies behind the thyroid gland. Therefore, when removing the thyroid, we had to safeguard this nerve and make sure we don't damage it. There are four very small glands called the parathyroid glands at the back of the thyroid gland. These control the calcium levels in the blood, and you have to be very careful to not damage or remove them accidentally or patients will have problems with their calcium levels. Last but not least, the internal carotid arteries, one on each side of the neck, which supply the brain with oxygenated blood. So, you can see my concern about this operation.

On one occasion in the early stage of my career, I was assisting a consultant and I watched as he divided (cut through) the internal carotid artery and blood spurted out with such a force, I was shocked. I have to say the consultant kept calm and clamped the artery and called in another surgeon, with a special interest in vascular surgery. He joined the two ends together and luckily the patient had no complications, but this experience left an impression on me.

By now, I was coming to the end of my general surgery post, but I was fortunate that I could now perform most surgeries with confidence. In fact, one day a new consultant, who had just joined the team at Blackburn was going to operate on a six-week-old baby with pyloric stenosis. In a new born baby, sometimes the outlet of the stomach called the pylorus, is thickened and narrowed, this causes a blockage and even milk cannot pass into the intestine. This condition is more common in first born male babies for some reason. Diagnosis can be made from the baby's history and examination. It presents with the baby vomiting after a feed and as a result is always hungry as no milk is going into the intestine for absorption. With pyloric stenosis the way the baby vomits is usually projectile and can travel several feet, this is a classic sign. You can also see an increase in peristalsis or ripple movements in the stomach and sometimes you can feel a little lump just above the umbilical (belly button) area and the baby could be constipated. All these symptoms and signs, make it easy to diagnose. On this particular day, this new consultant had a baby on his list, but he had never performed this operation (Ramstedt's Procedure) before. Of course, he knew how to do it but had no practical experience, so he asked me if I had done any and I said yes, I had done a few. He asked if I could give him a hand, the operation is usually straight forward if done correctly.

In this operation, you make a small incision to enter the abdomen and you can feel the thickened muscle in the pylorus. All you need to do is very gently split the outer layer and the muscle layer without making a hole in the inner layer, which is called the mucosa and ask the anaesthetist to put the nasogastric tube through the patient's nose into their stomach, then ask him to push some water through the tube into the stomach and if you see water going through and there's no leak, then you close to the abdominal wound. If there is a leak that can happen sometimes then it can be closed with the suture. This can really be a wonderful operation because there are no problems in the future and without the operation starvation and worse could happen. It is life-saving. Needless to say, the consultant was fine and the operation a success.

While as I was still working in the general surgery department, I had two very interesting patients.

One night, when I was on-call I got a phone call from a local general practitioner, he was concerned about a patient. This man was in his twenties and had abdominal pain, vomiting and been constipated for four days but because he had learning difficulties it was difficult to get a history. This man was being looked after by carers. I accepted the admission, and on his arrival, went to see him. I could not get much information from the patient, but the carers confirmed the history the GP had given me. When I examined him, I found his abdomen was distended, with increased bowel sounds due to increased peristalsis (the small bowel was working overtime trying to push contents down obviously without success). My impression was this patient had a small bowel obstruction, but I did not know the cause because of the communication difficulties. He had no previous history of anything serious, it was a puzzle, but I had to deal with this acute obstruction as it could be life-threatening. I arranged emergency abdominal X-rays just to confirm my clinical judgement, when I looked at the X-rays, I could see dilated loops of small bowel with fluid levels, but the large bowel was normal, that confirmed my opinion of small bowel obstruction. I arranged and performed the operation as a matter of urgency. During operation I followed the distended loops of small bowel down until I came to the junction of the small bowel to the large bowel called the ileo-caecal junction. This is one of the narrowest parts of the intestine and from this point the bowel becomes larger. I found where the obstruction was, a very thick object was blocking it, I still did not know what it was? Certainly, it was not cancer because there was not hard lump or mass and I was able to move it, so it was something unusual. I moved the offending object upwards from its position as that area would have been damaged if cut open where the bowel was inflamed and would not heal well. I held this object in the bowel between my left-hand fingers and made a large enough incision to remove the obstruction, and to my surprise found a large sock! Not a small sock but a thick winter sock! I knew he must have swallowed it but what I did not understand was how it had passed through the narrow part of stomach, the pylorus? I have never read in any text books or seen it before. I closed the bowel incision and sutured the skin and patient made full recovery and was discharged within a week with advice to the carers to be extra careful about letting him near things he could swallow!

Later I had another patient with learning difficulties who swallowed a rubber ball causing a small bowel obstruction, but by this time I had become wiser and knew what to expect and performed similar surgery and removed the ball.

My next post was as a registrar in urology, dealing with the urinary tract, kidneys, ureters, bladder and prostate gland and urethra.

This was a new area in my professional training. From day one, when I joined the urology department, I was at ease, whatever the reason, maybe because anatomy to my mind was very clear. Maybe because I had already performed a thousand or so of vasectomies in India? At the time, we had one urology consultant, one registrar, and a junior house officer.

It was the best managed unit I thought, everybody did their job well and they were very friendly. What I liked about this consultant, apart from the fact he was Scottish, and I had a great affinity with the Scots since my early days in Ballochmyle, was how he was very calm and had a relaxed manner with the patients and staff. He made us all feel at ease, I never saw him lose his temper, even in the most stressful situations. For the first month or so, I assisted him and watched him perform operations, then he started to let me operate and he would assist, this is what I call good training and I would never feel any pressure. I learned very quickly because I had the added advantage of having done general surgery. After two months, I was given my own operating list and I was very pleased with that. Obviously, things have changed a lot since then, which I will write more about, and my social life changed as well. One day, I was inspecting a male bladder through a cystoscope (fibre-optic camera), and this had a side attachment so you could show the inside of the bladder to the junior doctors and nurses. On this occasion, there was a student nurse who was doing her training in theatre, she was standing right next to me as I was sitting on a stool, ready to inspect the bladder. I looked at her, making eye contact and at that moment something strange happened, I just liked her instantly! I gave her the side attachment to look through and explained what I was doing. Luckily, the anatomy was normal. I did not think she showed any interest in me as she never made any comment or even said thank you. When I saw her in the theatre again without a mask and I thought she was beautiful, very slim, piercing blue eyes and long brown hair. I really liked her. I was not really looking for a girlfriend at the time, but this seemed like fate. I kept asking her for a pen even though I already had one in my pocket. Still, she did not show me any emotions, as if to say she was not really bothered. It did put me off a little, but my heart was set on her. So, I still kept making excuses to talk to her and by this time I think she realised that I was interested. I did not have the courage to ask her out for two reasons: firstly, I was registrar in the department and if she refused my invitation, it would spread throughout the hospital very quickly and I would feel humiliated. Secondly, I have not had a girlfriend for a while, so I was a bit nervous about it. I think she must have spoken to her friends, from what I gather she had really positive feedback about me from everybody. She told me later on when we started going out. So, every time she was in theatre, I asked for a pen or for my gown to be tied, anything to get her attention but I did not ask her out because I did not know how she felt about me. One day, my doctor friend and I went for a drink in a local pub, The Observatory near Queen's Park Hospital which was part of the Blackburn Hospital Group. Queen's Park had originally been the town's workhouse but later became a hospital. There were several medical wards, the local obstetrics and gynaecology unit, psychiatry and the paediatric medical departments as well as much of the administration for both hospitals. Now it is the site of the new Royal Blackburn Hospital. The old hospital, BRI has been demolished, but back then The Observatory pub was between the two hospitals.

When talking of the closure of old hospitals and being replaced with new ones, the Stonehouse hospital in Scotland has moved to a new building, my wife and I have visited, the old memories remain but my first hospital has gone. Also, the hospital in Merthyr Tydfil is now in a new building and called the Prince Charles Hospital. Again, the memories of the old hospital were still there but it was replaced, that was my second proper job in the country.

I finally fell for a girl

As I was saying, my friend and I went to the Observatory pub and were having a drink. We had just finished our first pints and it was my round, so I went to the bar. I was waiting to be served and I saw these two nurses sat having a drink, one of them was the nurse I fancied. I was facing the bar and about to order a round when I saw her standing next to me. Before I could ask her whether I could buy her a drink, she smiled and said mine's half a lager and lime. I was in a state of shock and all I said was, of course. I do not think I said much after that, I got her and her friend a drink. Afterwards, we joined them and had a good evening. Now I felt comfortable in that if I asked her out, she would be likely to say yes. I think I asked her out for a drink in August 1981 and she agreed but she still did not show any excitement about it, but at least it was a positive response. That first night, we, that was Heather, her friend and my friend left the Observatory and went onto a popular haunt in Blackburn, Bay Horse, New Inns night club, it was a Thursday night. Thursdays was always a good night there, back in the day. New Inns, like most places, has changed, I think it partially burnt down at one point, and is now an Indian restaurant called the Spice Lounge. Back then, my friend, Dr A, asked Heather to dance but sadly it did not end well as he slipped and fell flat on the floor, and that was his dancing career finished. He is now a retired GP and married with a grown-up family.

After this fateful evening my life changed, we started to go out regularly. The first time I asked her out was to a local restaurant, The Trafalgar, on the A59 between Blackburn and Preston. It has changed its name many times over the last forty years. It was about eight p.m. and had been raining, as we walked in, up a wooden ramp, I slipped and fell. I just got up, brushed myself off and in we went. I wasn't hurt physically but my pride definitely was. Anyway, we really enjoyed ourselves and soon forgot about the fall.

She used to live in the deck access flats at Shadsworth. I've never been a person who liked high-rise flats and that is no disrespect to those who live in them, it just does not do for me, in fact my daughter and son both lived in flats in Manchester. My daughter with her baby lived in a flat although now she has a house. Heather's flat was always cold, and I just did not feel that comfortable but that didn't stop me seeing her and her friend who shared the flat with her. I used to live in the hospital accommodation when I was on-call but went to my house in Clayton le Moors on days off. We rotated where we would meet up. Our relationship was public knowledge in the hospital environment. It was all going well, and my urology job was progressing well too.

Once, I jokingly said to Heather if you marry me, I will show you the world. Looking back through our life together, we have seen a lot. The first time we went on holiday was to the Bahamas, flying with British Airways from Heathrow in June 1982. I had booked this holiday and it was the first time that Heather ever went abroad. It was one of the best holidays we had. We went on a glass boat trip to the desert island with beautiful beaches and crystal-clear water under the cloudless the sky. The guy who took us on the boat trip left all sorts of drinks on the beach and let us help ourselves and swim while he cooked on the barbecue. This was paradise for a twenty-one-year-old woman, but of course we had both got drunk and coming back on the boat we were meant to see the fish through the glass bottom of the boat, but I could not steady myself.

That night, everything in the room began moving and I had a dream that I was Kunta Kinte, the main character in the novel, Roots by Alex Haley. Roots followed the lineage of a person who was sold into slavery and transported to the United States, and we had been reading this book which was why our first cat was called Kizzy after a character. In my dream I was trapped under some netting and trying to get out. The bed moved so much I slept on the floor, I think Heather noticed my movements as I struggled to escape! Heather, being fair skinned had quite a bit of sunburn on her upper body and ended up possibly with sun-stroke and spent three days recovering! Even so those were very happy memories.

Now I had my own operating list twice a week and outpatients lists, I spent one in three nights on-call and one in three weekends. I had no issues with my working life or personal life, I was really enjoying life to the full, but I had to think about my next job. I was about to finish my contract after the last six months here, as far my urology job was concerned, my consultant was excellent and I did almost all the major surgeries in urology, anything to do with the urinary system. One of the more common conditions were bladder tumours and if diagnosed early, the treatment was generally successful, but we had to keep checking the urinary bladder through the cystoscope, using a fibre-optic camera that is in the patient's bladder, every three to six months. We performed cystoscopy checks to see if there was any regrowth of the tumour, if there was, we had to treat it with diathermy or dissect and cut it out. This can be good for the patients, it is relatively quick but sadly sometimes a patient would come too late and require more invasive procedures. Treatment then became major surgery often to remove the bladder. This was one of the major surgical procedures in the urology department. It was a long, tiring operation and it could take three to four hours. I had assisted my consultant a few times for this procedure. Now, I was allowed to do this operation independently with a junior doctor and a theatre sister assisting me.

Part of the procedure was quite easy, I had already done bowel surgery in the general surgery department. There were two parts to this surgery: firstly, remove the urinary bladder and detach the ureters from the bladder and delicately move the cut ends, put them temporarily in a plastic bag as urine can still flow and needs collection. This is because these are the tubes carrying urine from the kidneys to the bladder. So, they still kept draining the urine into the collection bag. Then we had to make the "new" bladder out of the small bowel loop, this loop of bowel is used with its blood supply intact and two cut ends of bowel are rejoined to restore continuity of the bowel. Next, we close one end of the bowel and in the middle of the loop join the ureters which are draining urine. Then the other end of the bowel making the new bladder is brought out of the abdominal wall to act as a conduit for the urine and when this is done a urostomy bag is placed over it. We also had to make sure there was no leaks from all the anastomosis (joins) we have created to the bowel. When we had checked all was well, we closed the abdominal wound. It sounds like plumbing, but it works, and the patient usually do well, except for the fact that they have to learn how to empty the urine bag and put it back. The other common procedures were for kidney and ureteric stones. That was reasonably easy but as I left there was a new procedure being introduced called lithotripsy, crushing the stones with a machine and allowing them to pass through the ureters, bladder, urethra and out. This avoids open surgery.

We also used to do prostate operations, initially it used to be retro-pubic prostatectomy, which was one of the bloodiest operations, meaning they used to bleed a lot. The prostate is a very vascular organ, but eventually it was almost replaced by trans-urethral resection of the prostate — T.U.R.P for short. This was to operate on the prostate through a cystoscope which is passed up the male urethra towards the bladder. It was very successful in improving patient symptoms, however one complication to watch for was to not go beyond an anatomical land mark called the verumontanum. Otherwise, the urethral sphincter, the valve which stops urine dribbling constantly, could be damaged and the patient will have incontinence. I was lucky enough to never cause this complication due to the rule of thumb, which is that you can always remove more in future if necessary but if you cause incontinence, it can be difficult to correct.

We also did other urological procedures such as nephrectomies (removing kidneys). This was most commonly for a cancer called renal cell carcinoma. If it is detected early, it can be very successful. Removal of a kidney is reasonably easy, except you have to be careful not to damage the small adrenal glands on the upper pole of each kidney. These are very important because they produce the hormones cortisol, aldosterone, adrenaline and noradrenaline. We cannot live without these hormones. The removal of one kidney is no problem you can live with one healthy kidney. There is another type of kidney cancer called transitional cell cancer which arises from the lining of the urinary tract and treatment is quite different because if it is from the lining it can re-occur anywhere in the whole urinary tract, from the kidney, ureter, bladder and urethra therefore, we watch for these in the future after treatment.

In urology we also used to do a procedure called Anderson-Hynes pyeloplasty for narrowing of the pelviureteric junction because it causes obstruction to urine flow from the kidneys to the bladder. The result of this procedure was generally good.

There were other procedures we did for the scrotum and testes, apart from removal of fluid around the testes (hydrocele) and circumcision. We did operations for testicular cancer, but the most important point is that treatment is very successful if diagnosed and treated early, and even sometimes late, compared to other cancers.

As I was doing my job in urology, I was also thinking about what to do next. I had a few options:

I had already passed the American medical entrance examination a couple years before. I had gone to Liverpool for the examination. It was like my final year MBBS medical college examination. It was called ECFMG. The only problem with that was I would have to start from the bottom again, with a first-year residency. They had a system called the residency program and it takes you about five years, then you graduate as a surgeon, but I did not like that idea.

By summer 1982, Heather was by now living with me at Clayton Le Moors. We still went out for meals fairly regularly. One day, in early 1983 we went out for a drink in a pub by the canal. After we finished and we were walking by the canal, Heather seemed to be in a thoughtful and serious mood, I could see that. Eventually she asked me what my plans were for the future. I said that I had none and that I did not really have any idea. She went on and said that we have been going out for a while now, but we have no plans made for our future, like marriage and that shocked me. I had not really given any thought to it. I just said I am not sure or something like that. She just said, 'I want to know whether you are serious about settling down.' To me, it was obvious that I wanted to be with her, but she was not happy about this situation. 'I need to know,' she said.

'Well,' I said, 'we will get engaged, that's commitment.' She was happy about this idea and sort of relaxed after that. Within a short period, we went ring shopping at Preston's of Bolton and I let her choose, that is what she wanted. We finally got engaged on the 1st of April 1983, and celebrated, but without either of our parents joining us.

Back to my career, as an alternative to America I could apply for a job in one of the Middle Eastern countries because the salary was quite high, then go back to India and start work there. My cousins did this and it was a good career move for them. I had an interview to work in Saudi Arabia, this took place in Manchester, but there were two problems. I found out that the Saudi government took your passport away when you go to work there and give it back when you leave, at least that's how it was in 1981. Also, you can't drink alcohol there, Saudi Arabia has a strict no alcohol policy and I respect their law, but I liked my freedom to drink so that was that, I gave up on that idea.

I decided to apply for another registrar job, whilst Heather and I decided what to do about our future. I didn't think I would have any difficulty getting a registrar post because I had lots of experience by now and good references. I applied for only a few, not like before when I used to do thirty or forty applications. I got a job in Lincoln County Hospital but by now

Heather had qualified as an RGN, a registered general nurse and was living with me at our house in Clayton le Moors. She worked in the orthopaedic department in Blackburn. That meant I would be away during the week and back most weekends, when not on duty. It was a long drive, but Heather and I agreed to this. Heather was very good at organising things and very independent, so we had no problems. Finally, when I finished my job at Blackburn, I had to say my goodbyes to all the consultants, ward sisters, theatre sisters and theatre porters. It was very emotional for me, because this is where I qualified as a surgeon, and this is where I met Heather. Leaving Blackburn was difficult, I felt at home there and the staff treated me as family. Once, one of our ward sisters asked me to put her son on my list because she has been very impressed with my operation results. I was very honoured to do the operation, and all went well. If I had chosen one speciality, I would certainly have chosen Urology. That doesn't mean I did not like general surgery, but the time had come for me to move on to my new job in Lincoln. I was sorry to leave the Royal Infirmary, I left some good friends and happy times behind.

1983 — Lincoln County Hospital

Lincoln is a beautiful city, it has a cathedral situated on the highest point. At night, when making the one-hundred-and-forty-mile journey from Clayton le Moors, you knew you were nearly there when you could see the cathedral lit up on the hill. It would appear in view on a clear night, about ten miles outside Lincoln orange lights outlining its shape like a beacon of hope, high up on its hill. Lincoln is named from the Roman name for the area, Lindum. The surroundings are quite flat with farming land. One of the things I remember about Lincoln is the country pubs. I used to order a porterhouse steak and chips but could not finish it, we always took a doggy bag home.

Lincoln County Hospital was a district hospital with two surgeons, one of whom was originally from Africa, I think Zimbabwe (Rhodesia). His family had first emigrated from England to Africa, but he decided to come back. He was very open, kind hearted and always there to help if you needed it. His unit included a registrar, senior house officer and a junior house officer, who were both local graduates. The reason for mentioning this is because in most of the district hospitals I worked in, I was used to seeing overseas graduates in junior posts. This was close to Nottingham University School of Medicine, and I assume that was the reason. It did not really matter to me because they were really good people, and I became friends with them very quickly.

My appointment as the surgical registrar was very straight forward because I had done this type of surgery before. My consultant assisted me a few times, seeing how I was, and then I had my own operating and outpatients lists. One of the operations he watched me do, although he was not assisting, a senior house officer was. It was to remove a ureteric stone, which was stuck at the narrow point of the ureter (this is the tube that drains urine from the kidney to the bladder.) This stone was causing a blockage which we had already confirmed by an intravenous pyelogram, IVP for short. We knew its position, so it was not really a problem. What you do is make an incision on the side of the abdomen where the stone is, then find the ureter by feeling for it you can tell where the stone is. Then you move the stone just above from its position if you can because where the stone is stuck, it could have caused damage to the lining of the ureter. It won't heal easily and quickly if you cut it open at the site, at least that was the logic and it worked. Once you have moved the stone above, you make a small incision over the stone wall, holding the stone between your fingers and remove it, putting it in a bottle to send it for chemical analysis. The next thing is to feel for any other stones in the ureter and close the small incision around the tube. This tube is called a T-tube and is put into the ureter through the already made incision and it has three openings to drain urine. One goes down the ureter, another goes up the ureter a short distance to anchor it in the place and the longest end comes out which you attach to the urinary bag to drain the urine. We did this because the damaged ureter is still swollen and won't drain properly. At first, quite a lot of urine will come out of the long tube into the attached bag after the operation. As time goes on, it will become less and less and eventually none will come out. It takes seven to ten days, then the tube is pulled out and it works. Mr H, my consultant, saw me doing this and he was quite impressed at how everything went so well because it was not his speciality.

In the evenings, sometimes, I used to go to a pub called the White Hart Hotel in Lincoln city centre, professional people used to gather here after work. We used to call it the "Watering Hole" because doctors, solicitors, teachers, and accountants all came here, and it was a good atmosphere. Then, sometimes, I would go to the hospital social club, where mainly nurses, porters and domestic staff used to go to but very few doctors. I quite enjoyed the chats and laughs we had whilst I was there. After a hard day's work, it was a relaxing evening.

There was a chap, probably around forty-five and already

divorced, he used to alternate between two girlfriends. He would bring them to the social club, one on one night and the other one the next night, but of course, I used to have a laugh with him. He had lived with both of them for many years, one had a caravan and the other a bungalow. He used to tell them he was helping at his brother's pub, so he spent three nights with one and four with the other. One was a nurse and the other a paramedic, neither had a clue about the other. Then to add to the mix he also saw his ex-wife on occasion. I had to remember the names of the girls on their nights, just in case I used the wrong name. It was quite tricky and one night I nearly made a mistake.

My duty rota there was one in two nights and one in two weekends, that meant I had to stay in Lincoln whilst Heather was living in the house at Clayton le Moors. I would go back whenever I was off, and she would come to Lincoln when she was off. After the weekend at home in Lancashire, I used to leave early Monday morning at six a.m. so I can get to Lincoln by eight a.m., and this usually worked. I would be in theatre by nine a.m. after a short ward round. This worked most of the time, but one Monday morning I set off as usual but on the M66 motorway I had a tyre puncture. I was concerned that I might not get there in time to start my operating list. I stopped on the hard shoulder and rang the AA, from a phone booth (there were no mobiles) and then rang Heather to see if she could come in her car and wait for the breakdown van and I could take her car. She came quite quickly, in the meantime I rang theatre and told them the situation and said I might be late, but I will be there as soon as soon possible. Luckily, traffic was not bad, and I reached the theatre at eight forty-five a.m. Then, after a quick change into my theatre gown and I was ready by nine a.m. That morning there were no complicated cases, so all was well.

In Lincoln, my accommodation was in a big old house, it had a circular centre staircase and housed seven doctors. It was probably Victorian and felt creepy and had a Gothic feel to it. A new doctor's on-call accommodation was just being completed, and most doctors had been re-housed when I arrived, so this house was nearly empty. The old house was situated on Lindum Terrace and set in its own grounds and as I arrived the doctors living there disappeared apart from one other doctor. The house was almost empty, and it was a waste, I thought. The bathroom was across the hall from my room. The hall was a grand gothic vestibule with a spiral staircase and a high ceiling. One night we rented "American Werewolf in London". Heather refused to go to the bathroom alone after that. I had to hold her hand and go with her. All things considered it was a beautiful building. Later we looked at buying it and turning it into a care home but while it was spacious and had seven large bedrooms it was in a serious state of disrepair. The circular hall terminated in a spire and all the various features gave it character. In the end we decided it was too large a project for us.

Life at Lincoln was going smoothly but I still did not know what I was going to do about my future and my steady relationship. I suppose I was trying not to think of the future and just carry on as we were, but someone had to make a decision and that someone did.

Heather's parents did not approve of her marrying an Asian man, her father had been very anti-foreigners, her mother, an ex-midwife, less so. She was used to working with people from different backgrounds so wasn't quite so adamant! My parents were not happy because she was a Christian girl who ate meat and fish, and it was against the Hindu faith to marry outside your caste and religion.

One of the saddest parts, with Heather's parents was they did not know me, if they had known me and then didn't like me, that would be perfectly understandable, and I suppose the same goes for my parents. They did not know Heather and although she used to eat meat and fish, so did I, and we are now completely opposite. She has been vegetarian for more than thirty years now and never drinks alcohol. We joke, she is probably a better Hindu than I am! This is one of life's mysteries that we will never understand.

Now that we were engaged to be married, I needed a permanent job. We discussed various options, even going back to India. I knew Heather was not very happy about that and to be perfectly honest, I was very happy with the British way of life and culture. I applied for a few senior registrar posts because once you are a senior registrar, it is almost certain that you will become a consultant. General surgery was one of the hardest branches to get into and obviously local graduates had a better chance, at the time senior registrar posts were rare and there were five hundred registrars chasing them. I did not get any interviews. I felt demoralised, I had an almost natural ability to make surgical decisions and operative skills, this is not being big headed sometimes you know what you are best at. Several years later things did change. Associate Specialist posts developed for overseas doctors and with a new shortage of local graduates more overseas doctor became consultants, I had just been in the wrong place at the wrong time. It was not an easy decision to abandon the job I loved.

We used to meet other Indian doctors around Blackburn,

several had moved from the hospital into general practice. In Blackburn, the overseas doctors all knew each other and there was quite a community. When I came back from Lincoln on my days off, we used to meet up and were made to feel very welcome. While in Blackburn I had become friendly with two doctors, a couple, both from North India. He was working in the ophthalmology department at the time but like myself had found progression difficult. Finally, he decided to join his wife as a GP. I used to ring him and talk about how difficult it was finding a senior registrar post. He fully understood because he had been in the same situation. He must have chatted about me with other GP friends. One in particular asked me to come to his surgery and perform vasectomies privately. He had met us at a friend's house and thought we could work together. I duly performed several vasectomies in his surgery. One evening at dinner he suggested that I should train as a GP, then I could go into partnership with him. He had split from his previous partner and set up alone and was building his list. His patient list was not big enough to support two GPs at the time, but if I was interested, by the time I'd qualified he would have a big enough list to take me on as a partner. That sounded reasonable even though there was a little uncertainty about the list size. It was a tempting offer, but surgery was still my vocation rather than my paying job! Also, I would need to do three years further training to become a general practitioner and I was impatient and thought with all my experience it was too long! The subject was quietly dropped, and I continued working at Lincoln, but the end of my contract loomed on the horizon.

Every Friday when the British Medical Journal dropped through the letter box Heather would scan the job section and send applications for the few senior registrar posts which were coming up. It had been pointed out by several consultants that registrar was a training grade, and I would be less likely to get these posts as I was trained. I could keep applying for locum posts, but these were generally only two weeks at a time and very disruptive as they could be anywhere in the UK.

One day, Heather suggested I reconsidered becoming a GP. My initial reaction was negative because I would have to give up surgery after all the hard work. Three years of training seemed like an eternity, but I looked again. I had already fulfilled some of the requirements of twelve months of surgery and six months accident and emergency. This meant that I would only have to do 12 months of GP training, with a GP trainer and six months of another speciality and at the time there was enough demand for GPs, and it would not be difficult to get into general practitioner training programme. Finally, I accepted that I would have to change my speciality and become a GP so that we could settle in one place. The nomadic junior doctors' life was tiring in many ways. Every year or so packing up your life and saying goodbye to friends you met along the way. The decision was made, and the wheels set in motion, it was a rather emotional time.

I was still at Lincoln and one day the theatre porter, who I was friendly with asked me if I liked horse racing? I said I liked horses because one of my father's cousins had a horse and I had sat on one, we went hacking on a caravanning holiday in Yorkshire and I also watched racing on the TV on Saturdays. He said that he would give me a tip and I should go and put some money on this horse. He said the horse was a dead certainty to win. He told me where to go to the bookies and I put five pounds on it to win. Lo and behold, I had beginner's luck and won thirty-five pounds at the odds 7–1, plus my five pounds back. I thought, great that was easy, well it is not as simple as that, or bookies would not survive.

Another time there was racing at the Market Rasen racecourse, and a horse called Browne's Gazette was running. He was trained by one of the top trainers of the time and was the favourite to win, but I forgot to put a bet on. As it happens, the horse fell and there was a lot of disappointment for the punters. The jockey, who was riding Brown's Gazette, was brought to our hospital and admitted for what I think was a minor concussion. Back in those days the nearest neurosurgery unit was at the Royal Hallamshire Hospital in Sheffield. On occasion I had acted as an escort when a serious head injury patient was taken by ambulance, there were few helicopters back then.

While I examined this jockey, he told me it had been a fluke fall and Brown's Gazette would win his next race by a wide margin. Well, that was good enough for me! In the next race he ran, I put money on and sure enough he won easily. That was it, I had a new hobby, and it has remained with me until this day. Heather and I have been to many races together, as she also enjoys watching racing. That way life becomes easier if both of us enjoy going to races.

I recently read James Herriot's books. One thing I have in common with him, we both missed our winning bets on the horses. James Herriot was given a tip to back a horse called Kemal, by the stable's head lad after Herriot treated one of his horses, but he missed putting the bet on due to work. I forgot to put a bet on Browne's Gazette when I was given the tip by the jockey. James Herriot's horse won 10:1 and he would've won fifty pounds, a lot of money back then. Browne's Gazette won at 7:1 and I would have made thirty-five pounds, quite a lot back in those days."

"The course of true love never did run smooth."
A Midsummer Night's Dream — William Shakespeare

While I was still at Lincoln, Heather was busy organising our wedding and we both decided to get married in the registry office at Haslingden, this was the nearest office to our home in Clayton le Moors. Although, I had no objection to either a church, temple or both, Heather thought it was best for both of us. She planned everything, the registry office appointment, reception at home, food, drinks. She had priced up receptions but a finger buffet at £2.45 per head at the Moat House was deemed too expensive. In the end she decided to cater at home, at our semi-detached house at Clayton le Moors which had just enough room for everybody. She told her parents but obviously they did not come. Later we discovered her mother had been in tears on the phone to her best friend who we both knew well, and she had offered to go over and collect her but as her father was so against our marriage, she did not want to go against him. She bought us an original oil painting she knew Heather loved as a secret gift.

As always Heather was running late, hardly surprising as she'd cleaned the house and laid on a buffet and then had to get ready herself. I was nervous and was planning to leave if she didn't arrive in the next few minutes. I have never been a patient person but this time it was a good thing I was! We finally went in. The registrar pulled Heather off into a side room. I never found out why until much later. She had asked Heather if she was entering into this marriage freely. The registrar asked, 'Do you realise you could end up abroad, just dumped and divorced?' She kept asking if Heather was totally sure it was the right thing. Now, Heather had taken a lot of flak from her parents and had stood by me, so an ignorant, uneducated comment like that was not going to put her off. To this day each year a letter is planned but never sent. The woman is probably no longer with us! We had thirty friends and family present. It may not have been the dream wedding, it was home-spun and low key, but it was fun! We sat about drinking Asti Spumante and laughing with those who supported us. Finally, Heather and I went to the Moat House, in Blackburn for our first married night together. A friend drove us, he must have been well over the limit. Heather travelled in the back, laid out on the seat laughing at nothing in particular. This was life back in 1983! At the hotel, Heather struggled to walk in a straight line and used the wall to navigate to our room, giggling all the way before collapsing on the bed!

The next day, hungover, another friend collected us. He'd polished off a bottle of vodka and was feeling delicate! It seems the other friend who had driven us had run out of petrol on the way home and it had all been a merry mess! When we arrived home all trace of the party had been tidied away which was a relief for Heather and the next day, we returned to Lincoln taking Kizzy with us for a working honeymoon! Kizzy was our cat, well Heather's cat.

So, our married life began, and we booked a "proper" honeymoon in Malta for the following March 1984. It was a quiet place, but it had friendly people and that is where I first tasted green olives. At the time Malta only seemed to have desalinated water and this made the tea taste strange. Malta out of season is not the sunshine break the brochures had advertised. We were cold, very cold we each had only one jumper which we wore every day for a week. Siesta time came as a surprise, every afternoon the shops shut. The pool was too cold to swim in and the sea too rough. There was "entertainment" at the hotel, a Thomson's 4T rated establishment but even my broad-minded wife walked out after ten minutes of the comedian! Needless to say, we spent our evenings in the bar and our days walking and getting hopelessly lost amongst the narrow streets. We hired a car and drove around the island, several months later a parking ticket appeared through the post. We hadn't earned it, it had been the hire car driver who had dumped the car outside the hotel. We both loved Malta and found the culture interesting and friendly. We promised one day to return in warmer weather, but that day was always put aside, just in case as we entered through customs we got stopped because we had an outstanding parking fine!

Before I complete my chapter about my time in Lincoln, which I enjoyed and always have happy memories about, I must write one particular interesting story about a patient.

One night we admitted an emergency patient, a man in his late twenties. He had been at a party with his friends, obviously they had a fair amount of alcohol to drink. He presented complaining of severe pain mainly in the area of his left lower abdomen. He then began vomiting and the pain had spread all over his abdomen, it was strange that when I pressed his tummy, he tightened his muscles to guard the lower left side, a sure sign of pain. When I asked him about what he had been doing leading up to the admission there was nothing to suggest anything serious, he was fit and well. When I examined him, to my surprise, he had all the signs of peritonitis and specifically there was more tenderness in the lower abdomen, we call it the left iliac fossa. I could not work out why a man of his age developed peritonitis and was so very tender. It is unusual for cancer or diverticular disease and there was no history of bowel symptoms at all prior to this admission. It was an acute episode, most likely due to injury or infection? I was puzzled, so he was sent for an X-ray. I went back to him again and explained all the findings and asked him if he was sure, there is nothing more he could tell me, because it was beginning to look like some kind of injury to me. I told him it was very serious matter, and he might need a colostomy, an operation where the bowel is fashioned to come out through the skin not the anus and a colostomy bag fitted over it. It was looking a lot like he had a perforated large bowel. He was shocked by what I said and started to tell me about the party. He and his friends had quite lot to drink earlier and were playing silly games, putting sticks, I suspect these were 'swagger sticks', up their bottoms and seeing how far they could push them. That answered my question. I explained to him, he was likely to require surgery and may need a temporary colostomy bag and at a later date we would re-attach the bowel. It was an acute injury and the bowel needed to heal. I told him I would try closing the hole (perforation) if there was one and I am almost certain there is perforation, but just in case be prepared to wake up with a bag. He accepted this and I performed the operation and found an acute perforation in the sigmoid colon, the lower end of the large intestine. Fortunately, apart from some bleeding and inflammation, the bowel was otherwise healthy. This is where your own judgement comes in. I had to decide whether to close the hole and do a diversion colostomy above the injured portion of bowel allowing the perforation to heal. It is not always an easy decision, sometimes a perforation will not heal, the gut contains millions of bacteria, so is prone to infections and if it breaks down, he will need another operation to fashion a colostomy and third operation to close the colostomy and re-attach the bowel. I made the decision, taking all factors in to account, that the bowel looked likely to heal and just sutured the perforation and closed the abdomen. I am quite sure some surgeons would not have agreed with my decision but luckily for that patient, and me, the wound did heal, and he was discharged without having to have a colostomy and any further surgery to put it back, it had been a calculated risk.

Now my post at Lincoln was coming near to its end and I had to look for a GP training position. When I was looking in the British Medical Journal, I found one of my colleagues, who I worked with a few years previously in my bachelor days, had become a GP trainer. I rang him and asked if there was any possibility of helping me with my training? He said he would consider it if I put in an application. His practice had two partners, himself and his senior partner. It was based in the Old Swan Area of Liverpool. Accordingly, I put in my application and had an interview with both of the partners, and I was offered a training contract. As a trainee I had to do a certain amount of out of hours work, this was a requirement. I accepted the job, and my change of direction began.

Leaving Lincoln was, as usual, difficult. There were the statutory good-bye parties and farewells with colleagues. This was particularly poignant as I was leaving the speciality I loved for a totally different field of medicine. On my first day in the UK, I had a suitcase containing all my worldly possessions, now it was two car loads and a cat in a basket!

The journey back from Lincoln was slow, we drove one

car behind the other stopping at the service station for a quick break. Where a strange thing happened:

Heather had started back onto the motorway ahead of me and was on the M1, while going back to my car I was stopped by an older man. He looked desperate and begged me to give him a lift. He said his car had broken down and he had no money to fix it and no break down cover. He asked where I was going and could I give him a lift into Yorkshire. We talked, he told me about his family and said if he got closer to Leeds his son would collect him. On the M62 motorway I overtook Heather, giving her a wave as I passed. Now, I have always been very trusting and found the Welsh, Scottish and English people friendly. Stranger danger meant nothing to me. Heather had a different prospective, but actually thought she was seeing her first real live ghost. However, I too was beginning to think my good Samaritan act was probably not my finest moment. My father had always been generous to a fault, and I prided myself in being like him. I would always give people anything they needed and pay for drinks and meals when I really didn't need to, but that's who I am and I'm not going to change.

I remember one time I tried to tell my father not to give money to people who had no intention of giving it back.

He said, 'Stop right there! Have you ever gone without anything?'

I shook my head and looked down at my shoes. 'No!' I replied.

'Then never try to tell me what to do. I gave you whatever I could, and I will always help those with less.'

I never dared raise the subject again. In fact, how things repeat, as I used to give my daughter's restaurant vouchers to some friends and sometimes bar staff from our local pub and our daughter found out what I was doing and tried to tell me off saying, 'Dad don't buy vouchers for strangers, they would be taking advantage of you'. I repeated the same language my father did, I think eventually she accepted it, but I'm not sure because she is very strong willed like me.

Back to the motorway: this man told me all about his business and how much money he and his son had and how much influence they had in the community. It didn't seem right, here he was penniless, hitching a lift with a complete stranger! In the following years I spoke with people who drove regularly, and I was shocked, people were carrying baseball bats and chains in case someone unsavoury got in the car, but I always feel for those who are down on their luck and could never believe anyone could hurt me, or could they? A cold sliver of doubt was beginning to expand in my head. I told the man my wife was in the car behind and if I pulled off into Leeds she would have to follow and would be worrying, so could I drop him at the services near Leeds. He nodded, happy to have got as far as he had. I pulled into the services and the man shook my hand and went with some change I'd given him to phone his son. Heather pulled up and ran over, confused and bewildered. I assured her the man was real, no, I had not been "car-napped". I also had to promise her never to pick up random strangers in service stations even if they had plausible tales.

1984 General Practitioner Training, Old Swan, Liverpool
At this particular time in 1984 there were few rental properties available and for the first few weeks I drove from Clayton le Moors to Liverpool every day. We had put the house in

Clayton le Moors up for sale, but this was a time also, when sales were slow and house prices in the area dropped. Heather and I decided we could afford to buy a small house in Liverpool, rather than rent for twelve months. In hindsight, it was the worst decision we ever made. I could've stayed at our house and travelled every day and stayed in a hotel overnight on the days I was on call, which was one in three nights. It would have been fine, but our decision was made. We went into Liverpool on a Thursday, my afternoon off, looked at five houses and we had bought a small three-bedroom semi-detached house in West Derby, just like that! Our new life had begun.

The job at Old Swan health centre was not that busy and certainly was not what I call overburdened but was totally different and I had to get used to it. My trainer and his partner were very easy going and I never had any problems with them. I did my work and also some minor surgery sessions for them. Once a week I went into Liverpool city centre for a GP training session away from practice, but it was all fine. In retrospect we could have visited more museums and art galleries and made the most of our time there, but when we had time off, we tended to come back to visit friends in Blackburn.

At Liverpool, the only problem I found was the night duties when I was on call. The practice in Old Swan handed all their calls to an out-of-hours service so I had no opportunity to fulfil the training criteria through them. So, I joined an agency, which probably was safer. I used to have a driver, who would wait in the car for me to return. Heather, was quite concerned about this night work because sometimes I went in high rise flats in Liverpool City centre and I occasionally saw patients who were not truly ill, just trying to get drugs like morphine. I never carried any in my medical bag, but it was difficult to convince some patients at the time. One late evening I went to a twelfth floor flat. The man was crying and desperate for a fix. He showed me his healing track lines and begged for morphine or methadone. I had been warned. Drug use was big business and addicts often sold on their stock. The drugs services had got wise to the practice, people would ring for new supplies. It's amazing how many dogs ripped up prescriptions or even spilt the bottles, or how many got lost or knocked over. The pharmacists were also to blame, they often didn't fulfil prescriptions, under measured or even gave glucose instead of drugs!! (Please note these were tales I was told to convince me to prescribe methadone or sleeping tablets or whatever they thought I would give them. I know it's not true!) The tales were heart rending and sad and the dramatics were world class, but I had been warned. The next stage would be threats of violence and actual physical violence, it was dangerous work! Then as a last resort this particular man asked for a morphine prescription, by this time I knew I was in danger and I had to make a quick exit out of the flat, it was scary. I waited until he appeared distracted and bolted for the door and down the steps! It was a good thing I was fit, and the man was already sluggish from his lifestyle. Downstairs the driver laughed, he was used to this scenario. He reassured me he would have radioed in to get police support if I'd been much longer! Heather used to wait for me until I came home, but time did pass, and work was going okay.

New Year came and went, Heather decided not to renew her contract to work nights at Fazackerley hospital but concentrate on her health studies open university course instead. Around the end of February, Heather found out she was pregnant. I did not know we were planning a family at the time, but I was pleased all the same but worried about looking after a child. I always felt that I would not be a good responsible father. However, it proved to be wrong as we did manage to look after the children to the best of our ability and without any parental help. In my view both children have turned out to be fine human beings.

Heather had worked part-time in Fazakerley hospital in Liverpool to get some extra money because for the first time I noticed my wage had gone down substantially. I had been on the fifth-year registrar's salary and now I was on a trainee GP salary. We had taken a mortgage to buy this house in Liverpool, so we needed money to cover this. During this time, I had to also plan for my next six months in a speciality so I could complete my GP training. I needed to get a certificate to say I had completed the training. My GP friend in Blackburn told me he knew a consultant in psychiatry and that he would speak to him about my next job, I knew getting in psychiatry was not that difficult at the time, but it would help. I decided to apply for a six-month senior house officer's post in psychiatry, yet again I had to apply for a job below my grade, but I had no choice as it was a requirement of the GP training. It was not too long since I had left Blackburn and I still knew a lot of people there. I applied and was interviewed at Queens Park Hospital in Blackburn. It was quite a big unit, with four psychiatric consultants, three Indian and one British. It was often called a "Cinderella" speciality, like elderly medicine as it wasn't generally thought to have the same kudos as general medicine or surgery so overseas doctors stood more chance of promotion. My interview was with a senior consultant who was North Indian. He was very softly spoken and well mannered. There was also a lady administrator, who I knew from when I worked as a surgical registrar, she spoke highly about me to the consultant, and I was offered the job.

I finished my training in Liverpool, said my thank-yous and goodbyes and left for my last job before qualifying as a GP. In the meantime, Heather's pregnancy was progressing well, and the scans were normal. After two years on the market, the house in Clayton le Moors sold. Now we planned to move near Queens Park Hospital, into married accommodation, in a bungalow on Haslingden Road, close to the hospital as I had on-call duties.

In the two weeks before the post in Blackburn started, we went to Antigua for a break. We stayed at a small hotel with chalet style rooms bordering the sea shore. It was hot, but we had a veranda to sit on and we could hear the sea. The only downside was a tropical storm blew in on our last day and our flight got delayed and I arrived back a day late to start my new job.

1985 — Back to Blackburn — Six months in Psychiatry

Finally, we arrived in Blackburn and settled in our new accommodation and registered Heather with an obstetrician I had known and respected while I was working in the surgical department. I had worked with her and consulted on various patients who needed both a gynaecologist and a general surgeon on several occasions.

One particular incidence stands out clearly. One night, I was on call as a surgical registrar, and I got a call from a General Practitioner asking me to admit his patient. He gave me some history about this patient. She was about sixty years old and had severe abdominal pain, vomiting and high temperature and her abdomen was tender all over. He thought it could be appendicitis. I accepted the admission and when the patient arrived, I went and examined her. I thought she had peritonitis, possibly due to a perforation of an organ in the abdomen. Sometimes you cannot really tell where the problem is when whole abdomen is tender and rigid all over, you suspect it is an infection due to a possible perforation. In those days there were no CT or MRI scans, we diagnosed by experience, and she looked quite ill. I thought it looked like a perforation but could not be certain of its whereabouts. We arranged blood tests and X-rays, apart from signs of infection there were no further 'red flags' on the X-rays. This lady needed urgent surgery, I explained everything including the fact we were unsure which organ in the abdomen was causing the problem. Until we had begun the exploratory laparotomy, we did not know exactly what we would need to do. Whatever it was it would be life-saving and necessary, she agreed and signed the consent. I "opened her up" and to my surprise found her uterus had perforated because of a severe infection. She must have tolerated a lot of pain for quite some time as the uterus was full of pus and almost falling apart. I had no choice but to perform a hysterectomy, remove the uterus. I could have asked the gynaecologist and waited for them to come and take over, but I knew which consultant was on call that night and I was sure she would have asked me to carry on and also it would save lot of time when the patient was so ill. I completed the operation successfully. The patient was given antibiotics in a drip, and she recovered fully without any complications. The next day after the operation I was going to tell the gynaecologist and explain, but as I was walking along the corridor, I saw her and told her what I had done. She just smiled and said are you trying to take over my job, jokingly of course. This was the same gynaecologist who delivered our children, and it is not easy to find someone like her. She was one of the best, not just as a gynaecologist but as a person also. I joined the psychiatric team at Queens Park Hospital. This was a completely new area for me and at the time still a very underdeveloped area of medicine. The reason for this being in the past if people had a mental illness they were shut away in an institution and neglected as if it was their fault. Also, mental health was still not very well understood due to the lack of clear brain function information at the time. It's not like other organs like the heart, liver, kidney, lungs etc, but we know a lot more now than we did then.

The main areas we used to deal with were depression; schizophrenic illness; paranoid illness; obsession. During my time even the language used to describe the conditions has changed. We had to do assessments and treatment of patients which was more like detective work than medicine. The way people reacted to medication varied and ECT, electro-convulsive therapy, was still in use. It was trial and error. There were some anxiety patients but mostly they were seen by GPs. There were also some chronic patients for whom the unit had become home, and the staff and other patients were family. One elderly gentleman was such a character. He looked quite unassuming, he enjoyed his food and was friendly. Sadly, he had syphilitic dementia brought on by, well, that doesn't need spelling out! He spent his days standing about smiling and using his catch phrase, "woomph" with an up-raising of his hands, he also insisted on touching things as he passed, so a walk down the road turned into him tapping every car as he passed. He seemed to fall through all the cracks and lived out his life on the unit.

There was another younger fellow who, at the time, never seemed to find a safe place. He shouldn't have been on the unit, but this was over thirty-five years ago, hopefully things have improved. This man had Huntingdon's Chorea, a slowly deteriorating condition where the person loses control of their movement, he walked with a very jerky gait and always appeared to be on the point of falling but, like a tight-rope walker, this never occurred. He had at some point tried to give himself a bath. He'd not tested the water first and scalded himself as he was unable to get out again, his family, at this point were unable to cope so the F wards became his refuge. He was pleasant to talk to, he was still able to talk and walk about but not alone but despite all he appeared content and was always well cared for. The down side was a bed was blocked. One other local patient made the unit her home. She was a retired "lady of the night" and had chronic schizophrenia as it was called back then. She had a wicked sense of humour and on a good day spoke coherently and charmingly about the staff. She was a character, wearing as much make-up as she possibly could, her moods blew hot and cold and it was always difficult to know whether you would meet her warm, but larger than life persona, or the street lady or the woman who swore blind the doctors were abusing her! She was well known to the police! On bad days she cursed a previous consultant who she swore had abused her in many ways and was frequently heard swearing his name at the top of her lungs. Now, there was a fast-food venue outside Queens Park, and she would often take herself across and proposition customers for money or cigarettes.

I remember one patient who genuinely believed he was a

Saudi Arabian prince. He could not be convinced otherwise. Some patients used to have hallucinations and delusions of all sorts. There was another condition called hyper-manic state, patients have increased energy, excitement, impulsivity and agitation. I gradually learned all aspects of mental illness and treatment and learnt not to be afraid of it. I also learnt about treating suicidal patients, my experience probably made me more cautious in general practice as I had seen the results! This was very helpful for me, as one in four or five patients in general practice have one of the mental health problems and I think it is still a neglected branch of medicine. The reason I say this is because if you have heart disease or a kidney disease you will be treated quite quickly but if you have depression, it very rarely gets the same urgent attention unless you are suicidal or a danger to society, for example, a person with schizophrenia. I was learning fast and enjoyed the work and got to know the patients. Some had been on the unit for years or were admitted regularly, giving them a familiarity, and I became a little complacent.

One day, I went to see a patient with quite severe schizophrenia with a nurse chaperone. All my working life I have always worn a tie but on this occasion, it could've been quite dangerous. When I walked into this patient's room with a nurse behind me, he just jumped at me as if I was his enemy, got hold of my tie and tried to strangle me. Luckily, the nurse and I worked together and managed to get away from him. We had to give him an injection to calm him down. That was a near miss, apart from getting away from the drug addict in Liverpool, I had never felt in danger.

I thought surgery was a much more peaceful, but this was my new life and I had to learn how to treat these patients for the rest of my working life, but I had no regrets as all people deserve the same level of care. It was just unfortunate they suffered from these stigmatising conditions. This work in psychiatry helped stand me in good stead during my general practice years, mental health issues often overshadow physical illness and with one in four people suffering some form of mental health disease my six months on the "F" wards was well spent.

1985 — "Unto us a child was born"

During my time working in psychiatry, Heather booked a place on the National Childbirth Trust classes in preparation for this birth and I am glad she did. We went to the house of the NCT facilitator, a nice lady who lived in Wilpshire. We had decided we needed to move closer to where the practice was and had been trawling all the estate agents in Blackburn. We liked the view at the back of this house, in the evening when the class started the sun was setting and filled the room with a golden light. It was then we decided where we wanted to look for a house around Wilpshire. There were a number of couples on this course and they were in many ways like-minded people who became good friends. We are still in contact with some. We've kept in touch with some of them all this time and we still exchange Christmas cards. One particular couple had two boys of similar age to Karina and Sam, and we used to visit them even when they moved away.

The lady consultant, one of the nicest people I have ever known, delivered our baby girl. We were about thirty minutes from Heather needing a caesarean section, so the consultant remained in the room just in case! Then, at 4.25 p.m. on the 1st of November 1985, we had our first child, a little girl at

Queens Park Hospital. She arrived ten days late. We were both very happy even though we had no help from either of our parents, we had all the responsibilities of looking after our new baby with no back up. I am sure there are millions of people who are in worse positions than us as far getting help from grandparents. We called our daughter Karina Sujata.

It was advised that Heather stayed in hospital for a few days, so I was left alone, elated and still on an adrenaline high. There was a Halloween party at the hospital, it was just for staff, I might add. The pharmacy department at the time did a little brewing. When I arrived, everyone wanted to know about my new addition and of course we had to wet the baby's head. My memory of K's birth day will always involve me rolling home, clutching a grey and white teddy bear which was about the size of a well-fed toddler. It was icy and a full moon shone down onto the ice, so I knew where not to walk. I had come a long way since that first job in Scotland.

We were still living in hospital accommodation, our house in Clayton le Moors had recently sold, and we were looking for a new house. We still had the house in Liverpool we needed to sell. We did rent it out but in true Jadhav fashion it didn't go smoothly. Two Libyan students rented it. They had a break in and claimed thousands of pounds of jewellery was stolen from the loft! They left soon after without paying that month's rent and leaving damage and trails of finger print dust in the property. The sale of the Clayton Le Moors house gave us enough money to put down a deposit on the new house we were looking at, whilst still paying the mortgage for the house in Liverpool. We spent four months looking and finally settled on the house we had first seen and rejected at the beginning of the search. We had stumbled across the estate when attending

National Childbirth Trust classes in the Wilpshire area of Blackburn, although we paid rates, to Ribble Valley Borough Council, so it was an odd situation.

At our first visit, I did not like the house, it was rundown and neglected. There were electrical wires everywhere in the kitchen. I think it was a DIY job by the owners, but Heather said that we did not have much time to look for houses and the house was in the area we wanted to live nice and near to the country. We can get out of the back gate and very easily go into the countryside. Heather pointed out, if you do not like the look of it in the present condition then we could change it gradually to our liking. The price was reasonable, and I reluctantly agreed, and we paid the deposit and bought the house. This is where we still live today and we moved in on the 16th of December 1985, with our beautiful baby girl, she was just six weeks old.

1986 — Settling Down and entering General Practice

This was a new chapter for our little family. Our first Christmas together at our new house, Heather's parents did not visit, I'm not sure if they even sent a message. Even so, we were happy as a family, Heather had taken a break from nursing, to look after the baby. Not everybody realises general practice was a self-employed business for all practical purposes. This includes tax, national insurance and you needed an accountant to sort out all this.

This is how the system worked: the government paid a capitation fee which varied depending on age of the patient. It was around £70 per patient but slightly more for those aged over sixty-five and again slightly more for those over seventy-five. In addition, we used to get an item of service fee for some of the services we provided, like childhood vaccinations, smears, health checks, etc. It was target dependent and that's why every practice had a different income. My new partner-to-be worked out the financial package so that it was fair to both of us, in that he did not lose out his annual income. The first year, I would get thirty-three percent of the profit the practice made and in my second year, thirty-six percent, and in third year forty-six percent and after that, fifty percent. The idea behind this was each year we will increase patient numbers so that we would not lose out on any income. I agreed to this, although, my income would be substantially lower the first few years. With me being a qualified surgeon, he suggested that I did extra work in my own time in the hospital on a sessional basis as long as the practice came first.

I was pleased with this arrangement and signed the partnership contract. This partnership lasted twenty-three years until my partner retired. We had two surgeries, one we called Ewood Medical Centre, near the Blackburn Rovers football ground, and the second a branch surgery at Larkhill Health Centre. The only additional problem was that I had to borrow money to buy into the Ewood surgery as it was privately owned by my GP partner.

One thing about my life with Heather, we never got things easily! We had spoken to the local community managers, and they were very happy for me to join. Ewood was classed as an "open area", that meant there weren't enough GPs for the population. The request for me to join was sent to the Department of Health, it had to be submitted no longer than a month before the planned start date. A week before I was due to start, we got the notification that my application had been turned down! This was devastating news. We had two mortgages, a nine-week-old baby and the prospect of no income. Immediately V, my partner got on the phone and set up an emergency meeting with the local managers. They too were shocked. It transpired two other GPs had applied in the same area and there was only room for two more GPs, not three! My application had been on the bottom of the pile. The local manager was apoplectic! My application had been the first to go in, the others included an application from a larger practice to take on a local man, someone from Burnley who had done most of his training in Blackburn and was well-liked. The other application was from an overseas doctor who wanted to set up a single-handed practice.

He couldn't understand how my application got turned down. A meeting was set up for the following day with someone from the Department of Health. It was an awful night! I barely slept worrying about what we would do. Heather had managed to source a childminder and was going to apply for any nursing jobs she could find!

The next day the three of us, the manager, my partner and I, went and met and my case was discussed. It turned out that as my application came in first it was placed on a desk and the subsequent applications on top of mine. The administrator realised it was their error but there was only room for two more GPs. The local manager fought my corner. He told them he fully backed my application and wanted me to bring my skills to the area. I was well known in Blackburn as a conscientious, hardworking doctor. The other candidates were also considered to be well-established doctors and they couldn't withdraw their permission to practice. The local manager told the official it had not been my fault and I was being penalised. Eventually, he apologised and ruled that my application would be approved but Ewood was now a closed area with an excess of doctors. I was elated and with New Year looming we celebrated more from relief than festive good cheer.

January 1986 Life Begins as a General Practitioner

I started full time as a General Practitioner and my new career began. It would last until I retired twenty-seven years later. Our two surgeries at Ewood and Larkhill were very different in many aspects. Ewood was mainly local people, families who had lived in the area for decades, like a village. In the Ewood area, as time went by, we started taking on more new patients, our list grew and the area we covered also grew. It was still a local population with very few Asian patients. The surgery at Larkhill Health Centre was built by the Health Authority as a new style primary healthcare facility, everything under one roof. It accommodated three other practices as well as ours. Larkhill stood looking down onto the town centre which was within walking distance. The patients were from the surrounding high-rise flats and old-fashioned terraced houses, erected in the hay-day of Blackburn's cotton spinning days. There was a higher percentage of people from an Asian background, the dependants of the workers brought from Pakistan and India after the war to work in the mills. The Asian patients seemed to be predominantly from the Gujarat State, which is north west of Mumbai. Most of them could speak English and those that could not, we communicated with in Hindi, even though my mother tongue was Marathi. I could speak three languages, English, Hindi and Marathi. I did not think we had many patients from Maharashtra, in my time I think I only ever met two in Blackburn. I do not know the reason, but I hardly ever spoke Marathi either at work or at home which is why I now find it difficult to communicate in my mother tongue. Even when I used to go out to meet Indian doctor friends socially, most of them spoke Hindi and not Marathi

My GP partner, I think was originally from South India, but he moved to North India, so he could speak better Hindi than I could, but the main thing was we were both able to communicate with the patients well enough. Initially, when I started, patients were reluctant to see me because they all knew and trusted V, as he was their GP and knew everyone well. He was an old school family doctor, the old slogan for the NHS was "from the Cradle to the Grave" and that is what he did. He treated grans and their grandchildren and all the ages in-between. Both areas had extended families, so a good rapport with the whole family was essential. He knew all his patients and had a superb bedside manner, he made them feel comfortable, I could see why they preferred to see him. I was a new-comer, an interloper and needed to work hard to gain peoples' trust.

Heather always said, 'To be considered half as good, an overseas doctor had to be twice as good and work twice as hard!' My belief is if you are good enough you can survive anywhere and under any circumstances. Our practice was a good unit, we had about eight staff at the time, but no practice manager, and the practice was growing quite fast. I was taking on a reasonable number of patients as I started to gain patient's confidence in me. People told friends and relatives and they wanted to join on these recommendations. This was good for both of us, it made the practice big enough for us to get a reasonable income. I knew it would happen if we both worked hard, treated patients well medically and also with respect and dignity. I personally never had any major problems looking after our patients and that stood with me for the rest of my life.

Ewood was a popular walk-in surgery, we called it an open surgery; this ran Monday to Friday and Saturday morning. I think ours was probably the only practice in the area which ran open surgeries, needing no appointment. It was definitely the last! Our Saturday morning clinics were also popular and less formal, the radio went on and occasionally staff would sing along or spend time chatting to patients. We would see on average twelve or so patients on a Saturday, saving visits and allowing workers a chance to come in. Larkhill patients could use either surgery and it was the same for Ewood's patients. Annually we ran an influenza clinic on a Saturday morning which always had the feel of a community party. Friends who rarely met would come and sit, chatting long after they had been given their jab. We stopped short of offering tea and coffee but with the colourful flu clinic banners and posters there was a good feel to the surgery.

I was working full time at the practice, we worked at set clinics, one of us at each surgery. Ewood being an open surgery was busier than Larkhill, which was run on appointments only. We shared the clinics and had differing half days. Out of hours we worked "one in two" with every week, taking emergency night calls and weekends.

Making Ends Meet

It was going well despite our Liverpool house not selling and we even reduced the price so it would come out at a loss, but we were still paying the mortgage on the empty house and our new house mortgage as well. I was not really happy about borrowing money. It was something I had never done and was not used to, but we had no alternative, we had to deal with it. I decided to take on extra sessions on my half day and also do alternate Saturdays when I was off. I knew most of the hospital consultants, having worked there for five years. I rang my urology consultant and asked him if there were any extra sessions in his department and he said that it would be great help to them if I joined. I knew how busy that department was. After a discussion with the hospital administrator, he offered me one out-patient session every Thursday afternoon and an outpatient clinic administering Prostap injections for prostate cancer patients. Prostap injections are used to treat prostate cancer and also pre and peri menopausal women in the early stages of breast cancer who are hormone responsive. I accepted the job after discussing with V, he agreed and had no problem with me doing this in my own time. He did warn me not to do too much and get stressed but I had no choice, and the extra job would help us pay both mortgages. In fact, I didn't find it stressful, it allowed me to keep in touch with my surgical roots.

Still, I was thinking to do one more session on alternate Saturdays to help with our finances. One day at a doctors' meeting the answer came. Having worked in the hospital, most local GPs knew me as Mr Jadhav, surgical registrar, I had performed operations on some of their patients.

JD, a GP practising near Accrington used to perform vasectomies every Saturday. I've already mentioned how I have done hundreds of these operations as a family planning medical officer in India. Therefore, both of these jobs, one in urology and one in the vasectomy clinic were no problem for me. For the patients, they had a doctor with a lot of experience. JD asked if I'd be interested in a clinic session, and I took it.

Now life was on track, both at work and at home, apart from the long hours, for both of us. Heather was looking after both a baby and the house and I was busy at work. She had also become my 'at home' secretary/receptionist. When calls came out of hours, she had to answer the phone if I was out and pass on visits. This was not so easy, in the 1980s mobile phones were a rarity. Often if a call came through, she had to ring the house I was visiting and ask to speak to me. The change of job had some impact on me. In general practice you see the same patients, with severe and chronic conditions, day in and day out and sometimes you felt helpless as you could not help them. I used to get very frustrated, I knew I had to accept that situation, but it took time.

Life as a General Practitioner
Evening surgery, often went on until eight p.m. I used to come home and take off my jacket and tie, say hello and head for the drinks' cabinet, get a bottle of Johnny Walker Black Label whiskey and pour a large glass with some ice and water. I'd drink one or two glasses every night, we rarely went out during this time. Heather used to make a meal and we chatted during dinner, played with our little girl and we both got her ready for bed. Heather did notice that I was drinking every night and it was becoming a habit, she was getting concerned. I listened to her, but I said I did not think I had a problem, as my work wasn't being affected and I never had a hangover. She didn't say anything after that, but my drinking was increasing, in that I sometimes used to drink three or four glasses of whiskey a night. One night I came home from work, parked the car, and came to the door with my medical bag in one hand. I was about to enter the house, when I opened the door, there was our little

Karina at the door just over two years old. She had the Jonny Walker whiskey bottle in one hand and the crystal glass in the other, because she watched me do this every single night. She knew that's what Daddy does when he comes home. He takes his jacket and tie off and goes to the cabinet for the whiskey bottle and glass. She thought she was helping me, but I put my medical bag down, took the bottle of whiskey and glass from her hands, put them on the floor and picked her up. I became quite emotional, I realised what I was doing was not only affecting me but my little girl too. I thought, what am I teaching her? Of course, I am not saying alcohol is bad, but I think I was drinking in excess. Sometimes I would drink a third of a bottle a night and if I had continued it might have caused huge problems. I decided to stop drinking completely. I know that sounds drastic, especially considering I enjoyed it, but I needed to break the habit and I did not drink any form of alcohol for three years. The first two months were hard, but I managed, and I am glad I did, and I am so grateful to Karina, who is now a mother herself.

When Karina was born, we were still living in hospital accommodation on Haslingden Road and every now and then I used to go to the Observatory pub as it was only a minute's walk away. One night when I went for a drink, I got chatting to a couple at the bar. We introduced ourselves, they were managing the pub at the time. They had two young boys and originally came from Yorkshire, but they moved to Lancashire with their work. We got on well and they asked me about Heather, and I said she was from Yorkshire, born in Leeds. They were very pleased hearing this because they were both proud Yorkshire people. They asked me to bring Heather for a drink and introduce her. When Karina was two weeks old, we got one of Heather's relations to babysit and we went in for a drink and after chatting with J and J, they invited us for a meal and that's how our friendship began, and after all these years we are still friends. When Karina was around two years old, they asked us to go on holidays with them and their two boys. We said yes, although by this time Heather was in the early stages of pregnancy with our second child but we decided to go to Disneyland, Florida, USA anyway.

1988 — Our first trip to Disney

On the 18th of March 1988, we all flew from Gatwick to Miami, Florida. I remember this date because during the flight our friend who lives near Skipton, Yorkshire gave birth to a baby girl. We spent a night in Miami then drove up to Orlando. I think we stayed in a place called Kissimmee, near Orlando. It was a multi-centre holiday, we spent one week at the Disney theme parks and the second week at Coco Beach on the east coast. It was magical for the children, people from all over the world visited these parks. The Magic Kingdom was the best for young children, without a doubt. We were having a great time and Karina was in her element. We went to Sea World one day and were going to see the dolphin show but Heather unfortunately felt faint and started bleeding. The SeaWorld staff called an emergency ambulance and paramedics put her on a drip and decided to take her to the emergency room. I had to follow them in the hired car, there was no navigation system in those days and the car park was very big. I had a great difficulty finding the car to follow the ambulance, and I couldn't contact J and J as there were no mobiles available yet. I drove in a state of shock. When I arrived at the emergency room and gave the receptionist my details, the first thing she asked me was how I was going to pay. She showed no emotion and gave very little explanation about how Heather was. That's when I realised how good our NHS was although I was angry at the time. In retrospect she was only doing her job, even though she could have showed a little more sympathy. I showed our insurance documents, but she told me they don't accept insurance, so I would have to pay first and claim off the insurance later. They did an ultrasound scan, and all was okay, which was a relief. We got the itemised bill, the treatment wasn't cheap, but that was the American health care system and that was it, but we were just happy the pregnancy was still ongoing. Heather had to rest for part of the holiday, and I was responsible for Karina's entertainment, but while we were at Coco Beach our friends helped look after her and she was fine. We finished our holiday and came back to England and went back to work, Heather had a part time job as a nurse and Karina was looked after by a babysitter near where we lived. Heather had been diagnosed with a threatened miscarriage and as soon as we got home, she was seen by her obstetrician. The bleeding continued for six weeks. It was later on we found out why. I was working full-time and doing extra sessions and my share of the partnership income was increasing.

1988 — A Little Sister Visits Briefly
On the 6th of October 1988 we drove to the Bull Hill midwife led maternity unit, where in the early afternoon, Eleanor Rajani was born only five days late. Everything seemed to go fine and, being a second baby, we took her home for bedtime. Heather had breastfed Karina without any problems, so she was used to breastfeeding, but this baby, from the start was not feeding well but Heather somehow managed. Eleanor was not

settling, and something did not seem quite right, and there was a small amounts of blood in the urine and she had a temperature. I asked my GP to come and see her, but he did not think it was anything serious as at this age it was quite difficult to diagnose. However, on night three, Heather had been trying to feed her. She woke me up and said that Eleanor's eyes are squinting and the pupil as moving rapidly, this is called nystagmus. I looked at the baby and I was concerned that she could have meningitis. So, I rang the paediatric consultant, I knew he would not mind me ringing, he told me to go straight to the paediatric unit at Queens Park Hospital and the registrar would see her and he would call in to see her later. An ambulance took Heather and Eleanor to hospital. When we got there, she was seen by the senior house officer, who later became a GP in Blackburn. He assessed her and decided she did not have meningitis and was ready to discharge her. Fortunately, the lady registrar came in at this point and examined her thoroughly. She thought Eleanor needed investigations and arranged a lumbar puncture. She did everything quickly and efficiently. Our worry about meningitis was confirmed after the lumbar puncture results, it was E. coli 0157 meningitis.

In front of our eyes, her condition was deteriorating fast, she was put on a ventilator and the consultant told us that the outlook was not good. She remained for three days in an incubator in the NICU — Neonatal Intensive Care Unit. After all the treatment they could give her, she was not showing any signs of improvement and remained on the ventilator but there was no hope and she died in our arms. She was six days old.

It was heart-breaking for us to lose our little girl, Eleanor. We arranged the funeral for the 14th of October 1988, a Friday.

Heather's parents did not come. It was very sad, even at a time like this their pride was more important to them than their granddaughter's death. The church was packed, and service passed in a blur. All our practice staff came, as well as colleagues, some relatives and many friends. We laid her to rest at Pleasington Cemetery in Blackburn with her great grandmother Hannah Glover nee Goodwin.

Subsequently, we found out Heather had E. Coli 0157 as a long-term infection. We believe Eleanor caught this E. Coli 0157 meningitis infection during birth and so we strongly suspect Heather got this from eating ham from the supermarket deli back in early pregnancy. It also explained the threatened miscarriage, but it was too late to do anything about it, we lost our little girl. Heather had changed, psychologically we both changed. Not long after, she stopped eating meat and became a vegetarian and still is to this day. I took some time off from the practice because I could not concentrate. Although we lost Eleanor, she will always be with us in spirit.

One thing I remember very well was that when we came back home from the funeral, and I got a call from a NatWest bank manager. He rang to tell me our bank account was overdrawn, and we needed to sort this out. I explained to him we had just buried our baby daughter today and I was not in a fit state that day, I told him I would come into the bank in the next few days to sort it out. He just kept repeating that we needed to sort this out but finally, he replied with okay but never showed any emotions whatsoever. It would've been nice if he could have just said sorry to hear of your daughter's death. There are things which cannot be taught. That's how some people behave because they cannot see beyond the box. We had overdrawn because we were still paying two mortgages and had a holiday as well, but I was not worried, because I knew once we sold the house in Liverpool it would be easier. Also, I was going into my third year of partnership which meant I would be getting forty-six percent of the profit and after that, fifty percent full parity. The practice was growing quite fast, and we had over four thousand patients by now. We reduced the house price again and managed to sell it after two years on the market.

1989 — Mending

Finally, we were concentrating on family and work. Surprisingly, Karina was quite resilient and coped well and within a few months, Heather was pregnant again but naturally we were worried this time round; you lose confidence a bit.

As for the practice was concerned, I was getting to know all the patients and had my own new patients and there were no problems, I was able to build a doctor-patient relationship which is so important in general practice.

Before Heather got pregnant with our third child, I was stressed about what had happened with Eleanor and I didn't want any more children. I discussed this with Heather, but she said we needed two children to keep each other company and they could be there for each other especially with both our families not being there during their childhood. I was still against it but eventually I could see her point of view. When Heather got pregnant quite soon, we were both concerned about anything and everything, she was booked in for her care with the same obstetrician who delivered Karina. This consultant was very kind and caring during the pregnancy. During this pregnancy, whenever Heather could not feel any movement from the baby, I used to bring home the practice sonicaid to listen to the heart sounds. This happened quite regularly. I thought this baby was very lazy and just wanted to sleep and not be disturbed but the heart sounds were normal, and this reassured us.

1989 — "It's a Boy!"

My work was going fine, and the baby was growing well, just a little lazy! Eventually, ten days late, Heather had another induction and at 5.25 p.m. on Monday the 20th of November 1989, Samir James appeared. He was a very laid-back baby compared to Karina. We called him Samir James. We used Samir as all the children had a Hindu name and James after Heather's maternal grandfather. Sam did not like the name Samir and in his teens insisted we changed it by deed poll to Sam.

Heather's parents knew about his birth but did not visit but Heather's sister always kept in touch with us. I liked my little sister-in-law, she's not really little, she's taller than me but quite slim. She is one of the nicest people you could ever meet, gentle, very softly spoken and kind and thoughtful, she used to come and stay with us. She had moved to London with her job as a radiographer, she subsequently married another radiographer and has two children.

1990 — The Practice Grows

Now I was established at the surgery and getting on with my GP partner, staff and patients well. My GP partner was very sociable. His wife, although English, was a very good cook and made amazing Indian food. He used to organise regular gatherings at his home with a mixture of people, some Indian friends, some English. That is how he was, but it meant we had to reciprocate, by now Heather had learned some Indian cooking and we did invite some of these friends and my partner and his wife and their two boys. I liked those boys as they were very well-behaved and had good manners, now they are both grown up

In the early days of the practice, we had an arrangement with another two GP practices like us. We covered holidays in a reciprocal arrangement for up to five weeks in a year but no more than two weeks at a time. That was fine but I was quite new in the practice, and I ended up doing most of the other practices cover and my GP partner did extra work at our practice to cover my surgeries. The disadvantage is that you do not know the staff or patients, so it felt strange, but because of the reciprocal arrangement we never needed to worry about finding locums. One day I was covering this other practice and had done morning and evening surgeries, but at the end of the evening surgery, the receptionist passed me an emergency visit. She'd received a call from a mother of a pre-school child but had not been given much detail and was asking for a home visit. That was fine as far as I was concerned because I had promised myself I would never refuse or postpone a visit for a child. However, I would have liked a bit more detail so I could have a rough idea of how urgent it was. Nevertheless, I finished surgery, did all the paperwork, signed the prescriptions and set off for the visit. It was not that far from the surgery, and it probably would have been quicker for her to bring the child. I visited and asked mother a few questions and apart from a low-grade temperature there were no other symptoms. When I examined the child he was alert, not crying, his throat a little red but his ears looked normal. There was no neck stiffness, photophobia or rash to suggest meningitis.

Photophobia is the name for when light hurts the eyes and you involuntarily shut them or turn away from the light source. His lungs were clear, and the abdomen was not tender. There were no signs of anything serious at this stage. I explained all this to the mother and if I remember correctly, she was living on her own. I gave her a prescription for liquid paracetamol, but I also gave her some sachets from my bag just in case she could not get the prescription. I told her, if the child's temperature does not settle or gets higher and the child starts crying and becomes "fussy" or vomits or develops a rash, ring the emergency number and I would come again. I thought she understood but looking back, I don't think she took in all the information.

The next day I went back to surgery and checked if there had been any out-of-hours calls but there were none, then I did my surgery. When I finished, I remembered the child from the previous evening and the mother who seemed a little vague. My gut instinct told me to ring her just to check. When I asked her how the child was, she said very calmly that he had not settled during the night was not drinking anything plus he was burning up. Without any further questioning I told her I was on my way and would be there in a few minutes. I was genuinely concerned about the child, as the door was open, I went straight in. I had one look at the child, he looked hot and bothered and was screaming like he was in pain. Small children cannot tell you if they have a headache, certainly not at that age. He had a petechial rash over his legs, it could be seen very easily and some on his lower abdomen. Petechial rash looks like bruising and these rashes are due to breakdown of small capillary blood vessels under your skin. When you press on them, they do not blanch or go white. I did not have to do those tests as I knew what the cause was if you put all the symptoms and signs together. It was almost certainly meningitis. I rang 999 and explained the child had suspected meningitis and needed an urgent ambulance and admission. The ambulance was there within minutes, and he was in Queens Park Hospital within ten minutes, this hospital was really close by and had a children's medical unit. This was a very close call and almost a disaster for the child, but he recovered completely, except for minor hearing loss in one ear. Meningitis is one of the conditions you need to diagnose and treat early otherwise there are severe complications, and in some cases, death.

There are various types of bacterial meningitis: meningococcal, pneumococcal, tuberculosis, group B streptococcal and E. coli meningitis are the most common. Meningococcal infection is the most common cause of bacterial meningitis and septicaemia. Septicaemia, now called sepsis, is when there is an infection, and it has spread into the blood.

The common strains of meningococcal meningitis are meningococcal A, B, C, W and Y. There are vaccines available against meningitis B and C which are given routinely to babies. Meningitis ACWY vaccine is also available and given to young teenagers, sixth formers and students going to university for the first time. It is also given to travellers. There is also a pneumococcal vaccine, and it offers protection against pneumococcal pneumonia and meningitis. There are sometimes cases of viral meningitis, but they are not usually as serious as bacterial meningitis. Certainly, all doctors, no matter which speciality, should be aware of the early signs and symptoms of bacterial meningitis. I would certainly recommend a precautionary second opinion rather than taking a risk and getting advice if you are not sure, it can be a question of life or death.

You think you are doing well and then all of a sudden, a case like this wakes you up. I always believe in following your gut instinct, if I had not contacted the mother who did not realise to contact me, how could I have forgiven myself if I'd missed the opportunity to help and I am glad I did, and the child's life was saved.

I had by now achieved full partnership and received fifty percent of the profit from the practice. Our patient numbers had grown substantially so we had a good income, and we were both very happy at how the practice was performing. His plan of expanding the practice worked well. We had to increase our staffing level accordingly, but we still did not have a practice manager in the practice. We had a practice nurse and reception staff but no manager. One day, the senior receptionist who had been in the practice since V started working as a single-handed GP, was looking for career progression. She had applied for a practice managers job at another practice and been offered interview or the job I am not entirely sure. She had told V and he said fine, that's that! She was upset as she didn't want to leave. She came to my consulting room and became tearful as she told me about what had happened. I got the impression what she really wanted was for us to offer her a promotion. She said she was going to have to leave to go to this other practice and in truth she didn't want to. I asked if she'd spoken to V. She said she had, and he just said fine. I said to her, you've been here quite a long time and I suppose if we send you for some training, you could be the practice manager here. I said let me discuss this and see if we can agree to keep you here. I spoke to V, as I said, he was very reasonable and listened to my proposition and agreed if we wanted to progress, we needed a practice manager. This receptionist was not quite ready, she had no prior management experience or training, but we could give her some training and we knew she was hard-working and kind-hearted, so we appointed her. Now we could afford to, we increased her pay level along with all the other staff and the whole team was happy.

All general practices are run as a private business but not all practices had the same facilities, but we offered minor surgery and vasectomies. This meant that at our practice, patients did not have to wait for the removal of skin lesions and biopsies of minor lumps and bumps. I started two clinics in the practice, one for minor surgery and cryosurgery for warts. We had to buy a machine and liquid nitrogen to freeze the viral warts. This way we both brought our practice to excellent standards and the majority of the patients were very happy, in our practice patient satisfaction survey, we achieved an over ninety-five percent satisfaction rate.

Now our practice was beginning to look like a practice should be. We had open surgery six days a week, so nobody had to wait to see a doctor. Our patient list had doubled from when I joined the practice. We started with two thousand and seven hundred patients and now we had five thousand and four hundred patients in six years. We had to stop taking new patients and if anybody wanted to join, they could go on a waiting list. Our list target was a maximum of five thousand and five hundred, otherwise we could not give the best service. At least we were happy with what we were doing, and the patients seemed to be happy, it was rare for patients to leave a practice because of dissatisfaction, it was usually that they were moving away. In fact, when patients moved area, several came and asked whether they could stay on the list. We had patients in Chorley, Clayton le Dale, Preston and we had to explain to them that we will keep them on the list as long as they accept that we might not be able to do visits in emergencies and most of them accepted so that they could stay with us and that told us a lot about our practice.

Family Life
Our children were growing up fast and in 1990 Karina started school. We looked at different school options and decided on Westholme and we enrolled Karina there at Billinge House, the infant school on Preston New Road. It was a school with a good mix of ethnic backgrounds, few schools in Blackburn had Hindu students and whilst our two were christened into the Church of England, we felt diversity was important. It was easy for me, as the school was on the way to work, so when Karina started school, the routine was set up. Karina was so different as a child compared to Sam, at four years of age she used to get up, have a shower and put her uniform on herself and get ready for school every day. She used to wait for me at the door with her schoolbag. Sometimes she had her moods and could be difficult. One day Heather was trying to get her ready and gave her Weetabix for breakfast, but Karina would not eat it and just kept messing about and next thing I saw was Weetabix on Karina's head and you can imagine aftermath of that. I must say I was quite shocked but kept out of the way, thinking I am glad it wasn't me. Another time Karina was refusing to tidy up and threw a tantrum, so Heather pretended to ring a home for naughty children and get her a room with a little girl who scratched and spat. She packed a bag and

"arranged' a taxi and told K to wait by the door. It may sound extreme, but K had my hot temper and a simple "behave" would not work. Needless to say, she cried and apologised, and we allowed her to stay! Now all this sounds very cruel, but I knew Heather was a good mother and certainly did not behave in any shape or form cruelly, otherwise I would have said something. She was just trying to teach them discipline, of course some parents might not agree with that approach. I have seen when families have not disciplined their children and in my view their behaviour was not acceptable in some social circumstances but that's their way of dealing with their children. There is no right or wrong way to bring up children, as long as you are not intentionally hurting them. In our case both children have grown up reasonably well adjusted, and Karina has become excellent mother herself.

When I used to take Karina to school on the way I used to teach her the times tables. She became quite good at it and could do times tables up to twenty without trouble. She always wanted to be the first to arrive at school so she could play on the rocking horse in the kindergarten classroom.

As for Sam, he was more laid back and just used to sit or lie down on the settee and watch TV. When he was young, he used to lie on the settee so much his head wore a hole in the sofa arm. However, I'm not sure I am correct here as I sat and watched some of the old videos recently, from when he was young, and he seemed to be quite active and enjoying running around. I think I must have missed some of this because I worked long hours.

Both our children knew I was the soft parent but there was a reason for this. Since Eleanor's death I had changed as a person, regarding children, not just at home but at work as well, I used to be quite strong and firm. I used to be very good with children and they were very happy to come and see me. Sam was very clever, he told Karina to tell me she wasn't feeling very well, and I would take her to the shop and buy sweets, which I did. I genuinely believed it. On one occasion he said he felt ill and put on such a display, I thought he had a temperature, but I checked, and it was normal. Another time he was sent home sick from school. He said, 'Daddy, can you get me a Nintendo; that will make me feel better!' And I did, he was very pleased with himself, of course, his mother wasn't! I think she knew their plot, especially since Sam was the instigator. From then onwards, their plan did not work as well. I used to say ask your mother, but they knew not to. She was stricter with them, especially Karina, because she was quite the handful. I think as a child I was handful as well and my mother had difficulty controlling me, so I was told.

When the time came for Sam to go to school, he was not happy at all. He never enjoyed mixing like Karina and didn't enjoy play group. He enjoyed playing with other children but didn't like being left! Heather had to help getting him showered and dressed in great reluctance. On his first day at school, he had to be peeled out of his mother's arms crying, which was quite emotional for both Sam and his mother. He grabbed her hand, but she eventually managed to extract herself and the teacher took over. That was the beginning of Sam's education and no more settee and TV all the time, I think he would have been quite happy with that.

Since Karina had been nine months old, Heather had worked part time on the nurse bank. In 1994 she covered maternity for a practice nurse at one of the single-handed GP practices and stayed for seven years! At four years old, Karina had started dance classes for ballet, modern, tap and jazz, so Heather was busy ferrying Karina to her various activities. Karina was very good at ballet, she was in many shows with her dance school and took exams up to professional levels. She continued to do ballet until she was eighteen years old and could have qualified as a dance teacher if she had wanted but instead, she did a drama degree at Manchester University.

Well, as family life was getting busier, my work life was also quite busy and you cannot really relax when you're dealing with patients as you always have to be alert and you could not afford any mistakes, it could be the difference between life and death sometimes. You never knew when or where it could happen.

I'm now a seasoned General Practitioner

One day, a nice couple came to see me at the Ewood surgery. They had been to Spain on holiday and were both experiencing diarrhoea which was quite common after travelling abroad. I took a history and examined the husband first with no shortcuts, I never liked shortcuts in medicine. I had done everything correctly, but the lady said to me, 'Dr Jadhav, you do not need to examine me, you just examined my husband and we both have the same thing, a Spanish bug.'

I was not happy with this, as it was against my principles, but I did not want to offend or upset her so I told her that I was not happy but would do a compromise. I would give them both the medication to stop the diarrhoea and also asked each of them to take a stool sample to check for infection. Then they must come and see me in four days and by then I would have the stool sample result back. She agreed to that. One thing I am certain of is that if you are tired, overworked or whatever reason, it is very easy to take the easy option and not follow the proper procedure. I always tried to do my best. After four days they came back to surgery and the husband's symptoms had gone but the wife was still no better. I checked the report, but it wasn't back from the hospital. I rang the laboratory and they told me over the phone and there was no infection in the stool sample, but obviously it could be a virus like a Norovirus or some other gastrointestinal virus. (I do not think they were routinely checking for viruses those days). What concerned me was that he was better, but she was not. I explained the findings and I told her I needed to examine her, she reluctantly agreed. I examined her abdomen, then did a rectal examination. The abdomen was fine but rectal examination showed a hard lump within my fingers reach and being a surgeon, I have seen and felt this before, and I knew it was likely to be a tumour. I explained to her that she needed to be referred to a surgeon urgently because I was concerned with my findings, and there was a suspicious lesion in the back passage which I can feel with my finger. She was worried and then the questions came flooding: was it cancer, do I have to have a bag and how long have I got to live if it's cancer? I reassured her as best I could, and told her if it was something serious, which it could be, it did not mean she was going to die. If it is caught early, it could be treated and people lived years in my surgical experience, but first we needed to get all the investigations done which we couldn't do in surgery. She needed a colonoscopy (sigmoidoscopy), a fibre-optic camera which is passed into the colon for visualise the lesion and biopsy it, also an abdominal scan. I also explained she may need a colostomy bag. After they left, I rang one of the consultants I had worked with as a registrar. He asked me to fax a letter marked urgent for his attention, which I did at the end of surgery. She was seen, had a colonoscopy and a biopsy which proved to be cancer of the rectum and her other tests were normal and the prognosis was going to be good. I asked her to come and see me and I explained all the procedures, complications and the success rates. I tried to reassure her, she should be okay when it was all finished. I also explained about the colostomy bag, which is likely to be there for the rest of her life, but the stoma specialist nurse would help her adjust it, she took it very well. Within four weeks, she had her operation and was back home. I visited her and she was coping quite well. She thanked me for sorting it out so quickly. I just did my job.

People ask, why do we develop cancers? I do not think anybody knows the full answer to this, but what I can say is that there are certain things we can do to prevent it. Human body cells are dividing every minute of the day, in their millions, and new cells are forming and replacing the old ones all the time. That includes the skin and gastrointestinal tract, bones and many other areas, to form these new cells, we need the right materials and genetic code. You cannot build a building with faulty materials and it's the same with the body. In fact, the body is far better than some of the builders, to deal with faulty materials most of the time. There are these substances called antioxidants which stop the oxidation process and the development of cancers. Scientists have discovered oxidation can lead to certain cancers, but when the body is overloaded with toxins and faulty materials, then it cannot cope with faulty materials and develops a large number of abnormal cells, through the repetitive process and that is when we get cancer. We can help prevent it, to a degree if you can minimise the risk by eating the right foods and vitamins and minerals, from natural food preferably. What we do know for certain is that certain foods are helpful, like toxin free fruit and vegetables, foods containing antioxidants like oranges and green vegetables. Avoiding foods that have been scientifically proven to produce unhealthy toxins like red meat, especially in a processed form. I'm not suggesting you should stop eating meat completely but in moderation and certainly to avoid processed meat if you can. We also know that daily exercise helps to reduce the chances of getting cancer, heart disease or having a stroke. Stress has some profound effects on our well-being not just the mental aspect. Stress can cause physical problems by creating chemical changes in the brain and ultimately body.

Another question people often ask, is alcohol bad for you? Yet again we have definitive evidence to suggest that excessive alcohol intake can increase your risk of certain cancers such as liver, bowel, kidneys and urinary bladder.

Do As I Say, Not As I Do!

I do not think I need to say much about smoking, but it is one of the worst drugs human beings have discovered in my opinion. I am not a scientist and I have no authority on the subject, but I have seen multiple diseases related to smoking in my life. It is up to you whether you decide how to live your life, it's not up to me to tell you. Talking about smoking, I am not an angel! I used to smoke a pipe and the occasional cigar after a meal when we went out. When I was a surgical registrar, two out of the four consultants smoked a pipe on the ward rounds, in the out-patients departments and even in the changing rooms in the operating theatre. It sounds strange now but in 1980 it was acceptable. I thought surgeons smoked a pipe to relieve stress because of the pressures of surgery and perhaps I should start? To be perfectly honest I very rarely got stressed over a surgery, specifically my waiting-list planned surgeries. I did get stressed sometimes when emergency admissions for illnesses such as severe peritonitis, which needed an emergency operation. Sometimes we did not know the cause of the perforation or which organ, the anatomy in some severe cases was not easy to locate. The anatomy becomes distorted due to infection and the organs are fragile, then it can give you stress. That surgery is not a common everyday occurrence, but I decided to take it on board and smoke a pipe. It looked good, I used to smoke a fancy tobacco called Condor. There was certainly a euphoric effect as soon as you took a puff. It takes eight to ten seconds for the nicotine to reach the nicotinic acetylcholine receptors in your brain, which produces a neurotransmitter called dopamine, it is this which causes the feel-good effect, but it wears off quickly and you want to smoke more and over time you can become addicted. I only smoked for two to three years, my previous girlfriend had been a smoker so had never complained. Then Heather asked me not to smoke in the car, otherwise the car smelt of stale tobacco. It was the same with the house, she said the house in Accrington smelt of smoke. She washed the curtains, and the water was nicotine yellow! To prevent a recurrence, I decided not to smoke in the house either. It was a reasonable observation, I could not really argue with her about it. I continued to smoke in the garage but eventually I stopped completely as it did not feel right. There is a saying, behind every great man, is a strong woman. I do not know about the great man bit, but I managed to stop smoking.

Smoking affects almost every part of your body, I am not exaggerating about that point. I cannot write all the problems, if I did, I would have to write another book!

Talking of freedom to smoke, one day, a patient came into

surgery, he was about thirty-five years old and married with a family. He used to smoke a lot and I gave my usual advice about what damage smoking can do. He listened, then said, 'Thank you for your advice, Doc, but you have to die of something, and I would like to keep smoking because I enjoy it, if that's all right with you?'

I said, 'That's your choice and I respect that.' Sadly, he developed lung cancer at the age of forty and it was too advanced for treatment. He already had metastases, which had spread to his brain. Apart from pain relief, there was no other treatment then, but maybe there is now? His final words to me were, 'I wish I had listened to you Doc, but it was too late, I have left it too late.' It was sad.

Now I'm Old Enough to Reminisce
When I was working in hospital, I did not have to deal with management at all. I did operations, ward rounds and out-patients. I hand wrote notes on the wards and dictated the operation notes onto a Dictaphone. In out-patient clinics I dictated in the same way, and I gave the Dictaphone to the secretary and she (I say she because I never had a male secretary) typed it up. Letters were left for me to sign and then she would post them out to the GPs. As far as operation notes go, once they were typed, they were put into the patient's notes as there were no computers back then. When I came into general practice, I had to learn new skills, like how to manage your practice with a staff of fourteen. This sounds easy but it was not, if you have so many people with different backgrounds, moods, emotions, family situations it's not that easy. We used to have monthly meetings but not everybody felt free to ask questions or express their views. What I did was I

developed my own system. I used to ask staff members, at the end of surgery to come in and have an informal chat and get to know them and their family and ask if they were okay or if they had any concerns about their family or patients or even the practice. I used to say feel free if you want to ask me anything about the practice, or any family problems I am happy to help, and this worked.

One of the receptionists who joined the practice was quite young, very kind, caring and married with one child. After joining the practice, she got pregnant. During the pregnancy I asked her how her pregnancy was going and if she needed any help and said I am happy to help as I used to do antenatal clinics in a practice at the time. So, we had a Sonicaid to monitor the baby's heart sounds. She was sometimes concerned with her blood pressure being high and the baby's movements, so we used to do her blood pressure and listen to the baby's heart sounds and she was very happy with this. I know some people might not agree with what I did, but it was her choice. She could have said no if she did not want my help. Due to this, we developed a friendship in a way we could trust each other, and it worked. She had a beautiful, healthy little girl and was thrilled and I was happy for her. As a result, she would bend backwards to help me, and the practice benefited. I liked her nature because she was excellent with patients not just in surgery but on the phone and that's an asset that not everybody can have. Even after retirement we are still in touch with each other as friends rather than employee and employer.

There was another receptionist I had a lot of respect for, and this was because of her complete dedication to patient care. When she applied for the practice job with a small handwritten letter there was really nothing much in the letter, it was very minimal. She was married with two daughters. In the interview, I felt she would be very good at work, but she proved she was far better than I had thought. The main thing was that she genuinely cared for the patients, she was thorough and left nothing to chance. We were very lucky to have such a person in the practice, she was one of the best of our team. This is how we build our practice, of course, I cannot describe every member of staff. We were fortunate because most of our staff were good but of course occasionally you find one does not fit in the practice and we have to find a way to deal with this.

We had two practice nurses, one of them had been working in hospital just before my time but had a proper old-fashioned caring and kindness attitude but always wanted to improve her skills all the time. She used to help me with my minor surgery sessions. She had no theatre training but when I showed her what I wanted her to do, such as instrument sterilisation, she picked it up in no time and we made a good team. The advantage of teamwork is that she used to talk to the patients and explain everything if I had not explained as thoroughly. She supported me and my way of working because she trusted me and my work ethic. We made a great team, and I was very sad when in 2000 she retired. I did keep in contact with her for a long time after her retirement.

I spoke to all our staff one-to-one. This is where I learnt my management skills. I can say with confidence that every single member of the team helped us improve our practice and we all benefited. The East Lancashire CCG, our governing body, had a "Best Practice" competition and we came second, and I was very happy with that. The practice who came first was set up by one of the doctors who worked as my junior house officer in Blackburn Royal Infirmary. He was an amiable young doctor, kind, honest, religious and hard-working. He opened a practice in one of the more deprived areas of Blackburn, called Shadsworth. It was supposed to be a rough area, but we had patients there and had no problems, also some of our friends came from the area, who were well respected, professional people. So, it's just a label which was unfortunately given to the area.

Anyway, I was not disappointed our practice came second but some of our staff were because his practice won first prize and he was chairman of the CCG, the Clinical Commission Group, at the time. I still think he deserved it. In fact, our practice had achieved so much regarding patient care and satisfaction. We were asked to take part in a drug trial, of course it had to be approved by the Government scientific administration and ethics committee before we could proceed. We did two different trials, and those drugs are now used very successfully, one is now a mainstay even today. It is very satisfying to see the benefit of these trials. Our practice nurse helped me with these studies.

Life in our practice was stable and now the patients had got to know me well, so I had my fair share of patients and there wasn't any more that preferred my partner. Of course, they sometimes prefer one or the other doctor. It's human nature, we all have likes and dislikes.

One time a family made an appointment to join our practice. They told our receptionist one of their friends had recommended us. There was a man and his wife and their teenage daughter, who was about seventeen years old. I welcomed them and asked why they had wanted to leave their previous GP. The mother said they were not happy as the daughter was pregnant, it was an unplanned pregnancy. They had been to their GP, and he told her he would refer her for a termination even though she hadn't decided what to do. I asked them exactly what they wanted to do, the previous doctor had made the assumption she needed a termination without asking and they were not happy about this. I asked the daughter what she wanted to do, she was surprised she had a choice.

I said, 'Of course you have a choice. My job is to give you advice but at the end it is your decision.'

The young woman seemed mature and said she wanted to keep the baby and didn't want a termination. I told her that was fine and explained what we needed to do next. We talked about the pregnancy and taking care of a baby, her parents although older, and a little frail were happy to help her. Overall, I was satisfied that they had already discussed how to deal with the pregnancy and looking after a baby. I explained I would refer them to the hospital ante-natal clinic to see the consultant but most of the monitoring would be done in the surgery at our ante-natal clinic. Both mother and daughter were happy with this, and she had shared care during her pregnancy. All went well and she gave birth to a healthy baby. I used to do all the post-natal, baby clinics and vaccinations. We never had any concerns about this baby, the whole family were amicable people. One day this young mother came to visit me with her baby, now a toddler and she said how beautiful her daughter was and only here because of me.

I always felt as a doctor you might have your own opinion about certain things but that should never influence your care of your patients. People have a right to choose and make their own decisions. Personal prejudice should never come into it. I did have a doctor colleague who was anti-abortion, he would send any patients wanting terminations to another partner in the practice. It is my personal view that it is wrong to dictate your religious views on your patients. By the time I retired, this baby had turned into a teenager, and it was a pleasure to have watched her grow.

Circumcisions — circumcisions are another area where religion plays a part. Circumcisions are routinely carried out on babies at a very young age, most ritual circumcisions are carried out by private doctors and the majority go well. It is generally a straight forward procedure but sometimes, if not monitored properly there can be serious complications. Despite being trained, I did not perform circumcisions in general practice or privately, because when things go wrong, they could be devastating, and I didn't want to carry that with me.

Early on in my life as a GP I saw a baby boy who had a private circumcision and an artery had been damaged. After the operation the baby had bled, the bleeding had been quite severe, and the baby needed hospital admission. Sadly, by this time he had lost a considerable amount of blood and had gone into hypovolaemic shock. He had an episode where his brain was starved of oxygen, and he developed brain damage. Again, the family joined our list after this incident, and I was this boy's GP for around twenty years. He was the same age as my own son and I often felt sad for him as I knew he should have been playing football and cricket like my son, instead he was in a wheelchair and totally reliant on his family. When Sam was a one-year-old he had a bad virus and spent a night in hospital. This boy was in the bed opposite which always made him stick in my mind, we should never take health for granted or put our patients at risk by not paying attention to what we do to them.

Back when I worked in urology and after years of surgical experience, I once had an adult patient put on my list for a circumcision. He was in his sixties and had been having trouble passing urine. The foreskin had become increasingly tight. When I saw him prior to his operation I had been unable to see the urinary meatus, the hole men pass urine through. I do not know how he was actually passing urine. He was the relative of a colleague I worked with, so this added a little extra pressure to a normally routine procedure. When I operated, I found the foreskin was so tight and tethered to the glans of the penis. I knew even before I began it was going to be difficult but there was no alternative. I had years of experience by this time. It took over an hour to just to do the operation which should take fifteen minutes! I had to separate bit by bit the foreskin from the glans. It was a very tedious and slow procedure. I didn't want to cause more damage to the glans than there already was. It would be "raw" and take a long time to heal but eventually it did. Both husband and wife appreciated my time and attention. I hoped I never had to deal with such a difficult case again!

Mending Bridges

Around 1991, Heather's sister was getting married in Chelmsford, Essex. She had moved to London to work as a radiographer and her fiancé was also a radiographer. With a little trepidation we went, her parents had not seen our children and did not come to our wedding. I thought it was a rather brave decision to invite us. We went and it was a very good church wedding. Heather's father made a speech after and we went to the newlyweds' house where they finally spent a little time with Karina, she was five years old, and Sam was eighteen months. That's when our relationship with Heather's parents began to mend. When J had her first baby we met again at the Christening and went back to their house and Heather's parents got to know Karina and Sam properly. Sam was about three at the time and very chatty. Subsequently, we went to see them, and they came to see us. I assume they thought I was not an alien, I was just like them, except for the colour of my skin. I had the same anatomy and physiology as they did, and I was civil and hospitable with them. Our relationship grew and we started seeing them regularly. We had already seen all their other relatives because they were fine with us.

1994 — The Family Visit India

When the children got a little older and more robust, we took them to India and saw my family. We could not really do this more often, as it was a very long, rough car drive. It took us nine hours to drive from Mumbai to Aurangabad where we stayed a night, then travelled on for a further four hours. The roads were not that good, often being washed out by monsoon rains. I was concerned more about the children. I am not soft myself. The nine-hour car journey was difficult, there were no services or places to break for a tea and a toilet break. Heather ended up crouching in a field with a curious ploughman behind her, Caucasian people rarely travelled in these remote places. We decided to fly back from Aurangabad, the city where I qualified as a doctor. It now had an airport and good hotels. The plane however was not like those we were used to. There were no reserved seating, and everyone just piled on, first come first served. When you have small children, this is not ideal, and we got split up for the journey to Mumbai. We were half way to Mumbai before Heather managed to fasten the seatbelts on the children. That was 1994, things have improved immensely, and Aurangabad is now as good as Manchester.

On later trips, we stayed in Aurangabad and various friends, my sister and her family came to see us there. We visited some historic sites not far from Aurangabad. These tourist attractions are quite busy, some may consider them exploited. Back in 1994 they were much quieter. There are areas of carved stone known as the Ajanta and Ellora caves. These are World Heritage Sites situated in the Maharashtra State. The Ellora caves are one of the largest rock cut monastery temple cave complexes in the world. It features Hindu, Buddhist and Jain monuments and artwork dating back from the 600–1000 AD. It was designated as a World Heritage site in 1983.

The Ajanta caves contain thirty Buddhist monuments carved out of the rock, dating from 200 BC to about 480 AD. The caves were designated a World Heritage site in 1983. They are definitely worth a visit. Aurangabad is about thirty minutes by plane from Mumbai.

Balancing Home and Work

When I was a young doctor, I was in continuous employment from the day I arrived in July 1973 and could not do certain things which I can now in my retirement. I was one of the fortunate ones, health wise, in my whole career I had only taken twelve days off sick and three of those were thanks to our son, Sam. He was around six years old, and I was play fighting with him, I asked him to punch my hand. I was sitting on a chair, the game was I used to move my hand to avoid him hitting it and my face was well away from him. This time he missed my hand and hit my nose like a boxer. It all happened very quickly, my nose was bleeding onto the carpet, and I shouted for Heather saying, my nose is bleeding, can you get me a towel. She was outside and shouted back saying wait a minute I'm busy. I think I was more worried about the carpet than the damage to my nose! Heather came in eventually and looked at my face and said my Lord go to the bathroom and look at your face. I could tell from the look of shock on her face that something was not right. Part of my nose was completely out of shape. Anyhow, we managed to stop the bleeding and I rang the ear, nose and throat specialist on call and explained to him that I had fractured my nasal bones. He asked if I was sure? I told him I had no doubt, then he asked me when it happened, so I explained. The second question he asked was how brave are you regarding pain? I told him I could tolerate pain quite well. He said get here as soon as possible and go straight to the ENT ward and he would see me there. Of course, I knew time was important because the longer you leave a nasal bone fracture, the worse the swelling and the reduction of the fracture becomes difficult. Heather drove me there and the registrar looked at my face and started laughing, especially about the story of how it happened. He asked me once more if I okay with pain and I said, 'Yes, please get on with it.' He just clicked the broken nasal bones back in place but of course there was swelling and bruising afterwards. This got a lot worse that evening, so the next day I could not go to work because I couldn't put my glasses on, and I took three days off.

The children were growing up fast now, the school routine and extra activities meant needing lifts for the activities. Heather was working part time with another GP practice, and I was quite busy at work, but we adjusted our times as we could. However, Heather used to take Karina and I used to take Sam to his activities. His were mostly sports, either football or cricket, which were usually at the weekend, so I could take him and stay and watch. His football team was a local club, Wilpshire Wanderers but they played in competitions and that meant we had to travel around the region, but I enjoyed it and enjoyed chatting with the other parents. Then there was cricket, which was more on Saturdays and Sundays, or if it was mid-week, it would be in the evening. Again, I could take him and watch. We joined Salesbury cricket club as life members. It's a beautiful ground and the panoramic scenery can be stunning during a summer's evening. I started helping out at the junior practices and became a junior cricket umpire. When there was a local team match, parents took turns in providing the 'teas', usually sandwiches and pies for at least twenty-two plus people and this was a joint effort. It went well and during this time I met a lot of like-minded people, some of them became firm friends and I'm still in contact. Whenever I used to take Sam to cricket practice in the winter months at Saint Mary's college, I would go to The Sportsman's Inn nearby and have a drink with the other parents. On one of such occasion, we were having a pint and one of the parents introduced me to Warsteiner. That was a mistake because I became almost addicted to it. I just liked it so much, whenever and wherever I went I would ask for a pint! Not every pub stocked it and that was a blessing! It is a strong German lager and people used to say to me you shouldn't drink that, it's too strong but I only used to drink a pint or two, no more than that, so it was okay. At Salesbury cricket club, the gentleman in charge of training the junior team had been coaching youngsters for many years and he was an excellent coach. He used to organise cricket trips in Yorkshire and Worcestershire and parents could go if they wanted to. He would take the boys in a mini-bus without help but a number of parents went along to see their children playing. I went because I was helping with umpiring, as well as watching the cricket. It was a pleasure really to go on the cricket tour. At lunch we used to go to small country pubs. The people we met were very friendly on the cricket field and in the pubs. We used to meet for an evening meal with the boys. Heather's parents also came on tour to watch Sam play, both in Worcestershire and Yorkshire. One time in Yorkshire, near York City, we took her parents. As her father was getting slow, we pulled up close to the ground to get them out then went and parked. Before we even got parked her mother had fallen, she tripped on a step and ended up being taken to York General Hospital in an ambulance. She managed to break two bones in her foot and spent the night in hospital as her heart tracings were erratic. This point marked the start of us needing to look after them more. Fortunately, Bradford has good home care and before we even arrived back at their house equipment had been delivered.

It spoilt it a bit, Sam was a good slow spin bowler and I think his best was five for seven wickets. He also used to open the batting for the team and his best score was ninety-five at Salisbury. I thoroughly enjoyed those days and also became friends with so many people, even now on a fine summer evening I go to Salesbury Cricket club and watch the cricket and have a pint.

During this time, Karina was taking speech and drama classes and ballet, tap, modern and jazz dance and at various times flute and piano lessons and Heather was quite busy with that.

My wife attains the Big 5 0!

Heather was approaching one of her milestone birthdays. She was going to be fifty years old in December 2010. We discussed what she wanted to do. She wanted a family holiday which she had planned well in advance, and it was one of the best holidays we had. I took two weeks holiday from work, it was important to give enough notice to my GP partner, as it spanned New Year; we didn't usually take time off at Christmas and New Year. This was a three-centre holiday, we flew to Las Vegas for a few days, then to Hawaii for a week and the last stop was to San Francisco. In Las Vegas, gaming machines were everywhere. We walked place to place and played on the machines, I lost a few dollars and Sam excelled at Black Jack. Heather left us on the tables and wandered around the slot machines with a cup of quarters! For her actual birthday she booked a helicopter tour to the Grand Canyon with a picnic in that area. So, we set off travelling from the hotel in a stretched limousine to the helipad, surprisingly it was a reasonably big airport, with helicopters constantly coming and going. From our hotel we had watched processions of helicopters heading out. The weather was not great, it was windy, and the captain said that those of us who do not like turbulence should think about not going. He was not sure if he would be able to fly us into the actual Canyon as there were fast flowing up draughts. We set off not certain if we would have to turn back. Heather, Karina and Sam said they were happy to go but I was not sure. Then I thought if there was a crash and all three of them were gone, what was the point in me staying without them? So, I said yes, he actually asked me twice, but I had made up my mind and went with them. We set off, it was quite windy, and the helicopter started shaking but the captain was not concerned as he has been doing this job for a while. Karina, Sam and I were happy, but Heather was having anxiety, so she got hold of my hand and squeezed so hard my fingers were turning blue, she did not say a word. I could see she was terrified. Anyway, he landed the helicopter safely at the top of a ledge on the Grand Canyon, looking down onto the Colorado River. It was spectacular scenery, and I was impressed but Heather was not relaxed, she was thinking of the trip back on the helicopter. The captain put a blanket on a bench and arranged a champagne picnic for us. I enjoyed my glass of champagne and food so did the children, but Heather did not eat anything, but she liked the scenery. Well, coming back it was a little windy, we flew over the Hoover Dam. Finally, we landed safely at the heliport and went back to the hotel. That ride in the helicopter changed Heather and she won't go in a helicopter ever again. It's a pity because it was an experience I will never forget. The next day, we flew to our next destination, Hawaii and that flight was rough, the plane shuddered most of the six-hour flight. In Hawaii we stayed in the Kahala hotel, where Queen Elizabeth and many of the American presidents had stayed. We like to wander the gallery of portraits and spend time immersed in looking at all the famous guests. It is a beautiful hotel, a stunning beach in tropical surroundings, we could not have wished for more. We celebrated the New Year, there is a twelve-hour time difference between Hawaii and the UK, so we had already done all the Happy New Year texts earlier on. Hawaii is the last place to celebrate New Year. All of us enjoyed the evening with the pineapple drop at midnight and dancing under the stars. Heather even had one or two glasses of champagne which made up for missing out on the Grand Canyon trip, but the problem was it affected her, in a happy way. She started dancing and would not leave the dance floor and the children were telling me to get her back. If I remember correctly the words were, "get your woman off the dance floor" and we finally managed to persuade her, but she had a great time.

We hired a taxi to tour the island. I wanted to see Kealakekua Bay where Captain James Cook landed and was killed on his third voyage on HMS Discovery. I like history and find it cathartic to see the beach where he died, not that I like the killing but its historical significance. He was attempting to kidnap Hawaii's monarch, Kalani Opu'u to reclaim a cutter (crew member) stolen from one of his ships. This incident took place on the 14th of February 1779, and he was buried there on the 21st of February 1779. I am fascinated by James Cook's voyages. He was born on the 7th of November 1728, in a village called Morton in Yorkshire. After five years at school, he decided to find work and became a trainee on a ship owned by the Walker family at Whitby. He continued his progress and became one of the best navigators, surveying much of the entrance to the Saint Lawrence River in Canada. He also produced a detailed map of the New Foundland, and he did three ocean voyages aboard three different ships. First was the HMS Endeavour, second was on the HMS Resolution and his final voyage was on the HMS Discovery. During his voyages he discovered Australia, New Zealand, Hawaii and Canada. Although I say discovered, they were in fact already "discovered" by the indigenous people who inhabited them. Most of these became British colonies and were occupied by the British, after they displaced the local tribes. Without Captain James Cook to "discover" these places, the world would have been a different place. It is in a way; he changed the world map, but I am not entirely sure it was best for the local tribes or indigenous people.

I was interested in his discoveries as historic facts and wanted to visit some of these places.

I have been to Morton and Whitby where we visited the James Cook Museum. I followed that by visiting the Saint Lawrence River and went on a river cruise. It is very fast flowing and rough, but I am glad we did it. The last visit was to Hawaii, where he was buried in his final resting place. We stood on the cliff top overlooking the beach. Strong winds blow off the sea, trying to force us back from the edge. There is a feel to the place, so much history crowded into a small bay, the ancestors defending their land against the British explorers so full of their importance. The resonance lives on in the cliffs and the winds.

Our last destination of Heather's birthday celebration was San Francisco. We were flying from Hawaii and again, it was not a pleasant flight. There was a lot of turbulence and the lady pilot said she was trying to do her best by slowing the speed and flying at a lower altitude, she managed to get us to San Francisco, shaken but not too badly stirred. We stayed in the Fairmont Hotel, set high up on the San Francisco hillside with panoramic views over the bay, at least when there wasn't a fog rolling in! San Francisco was very windy and cold and walking up on those very steep hills was hard work, we did use the local buses and sometimes taxis. We arranged a visit to Alcatraz Island, one of the historic 'must see' sites. This was where the world-famous prison was from August 11th, 1934, until March 21st, 1963. The island is situated in such a way as to make it very difficult to escape from. It is believed prisoners died trying but I do not know if they escaped or died in the process. At its peak there were two hundred prisoners there. We thoroughly enjoyed our day seeing the prison and the island, it was a memorable day although bitterly cold. Now we had to pack our bags and it was back to reality of the working life. I'm sure this will remain in our memory as a special family holiday.

We Are the Club Sandwich Generation
As far as Heather's parents were concerned, we started seeing each other regularly and when we went to Bradford, we used to go out for meals rather than eating in. As time went by, Heather's mother, who was called Hannah, was not very fit physically. She had a number of medical problems and could not walk for long without getting short of breath and angina. Her father was not in good health either.

One of the things I remember about Heather's parents was the first Christmas they came to our house, probably 1996. Heather's aunt and uncle also came. Her uncle used to like a drink as much as I did at Christmas. This particular Christmas we both had a lot to drink, and I fell asleep on the settee and Heather kindly painted my nails. I do not remember any of this, I took myself to bed at about five p.m.! That was their first Christmas experience with me. The next day, I woke up as if nothing had happened and the best part of it was that Sam remembered. He was seven years old at the time and when he returned to school his teacher got all the children to write about their Christmas experience. Sam wrote, 'My uncle and my daddy got drunk and fell asleep and my mum painted Dad's nails!' What an embarrassment!

When we all went to parents evening, his teacher said to

me, with a smile, 'I believe you enjoyed your Christmas very much!'

What can you say? I could not tell Sam off because he told the truth, I just had to see the funny side of it.

I think Heather's dad had some sort of neurodegenerative disorder, and although the doctors diagnosed it as Parkinson's disease, we were never convinced! As far as I was concerned, without being arrogant, he did not have a typical Parkinson's disease, neither the signs nor the symptoms to unequivocally diagnose it, and Heather agreed with me. They put him on medication, which probably caused side-effects. Her parents used to drive to our house from Bradford but as time went by, they had a small crash (not their fault), and it knocked her father's confidence. Eventually, around his eightieth birthday, the car decided enough was enough and refused to go any further, which was probably the best thing! Previously Heather had asked him not to drive but I suppose he did not want to lose his freedom. That was the end of driving for him. I do not know how I will feel if I lose my freedom to drive, but I can guess it must be hard. The problem for us was that we had to drive at least once if not twice a week to Bradford, an eighty-six mile round trip, plus taking them shopping and out for dinner for a change of scenery. This was our regular pattern from the early 2000s. We usually went on Thursday and then as needed on the weekends. By this time, I had given up on my urology sessions at the hospital. We knew things were not going to get any better, but only worse. Of course, Heather's sister lived in Chelmsford and could not come up as often as she wanted to, but she came when she could and rang them regularly.

Our visits to Bradford increased as her parents' conditions

deteriorated but we managed, although it used to take a long time to take them round the supermarket. As they became more infirm, we used to go ourselves to do the shopping. During this time Heather's dad, Basil, asked me if I would act as the executor of his will to which I agreed. One thing he said is that he did not want to go into a nursing home, and I promised that we would do our best to keep him in his own home. Heather's mum's health deteriorated further, she had developed angina and needed a stent. The contrast dye seemed to cause a reaction and her kidney function plummeted and she developed renal failure. She saw several specialists, but nothing was improving her kidney function, she was offered a renal artery stent but declined, scared after the coronary stent. We were both physically tired and on one of these trips we both fell asleep at temporary traffic lights in Gisburn. The driver behind us blew his horn loud enough to wake us up. We were now part of the "Club Sandwich Generation", we worked, had the family at home and also the elders in Bradford. Eventually, a tipping point came, and Hannah had to be admitted to hospital to initiate peritoneal dialysis. She was barely eating and had dropped from size eighteen to eight in the end, and with bad angina she was weak and needed carers every day, but with one cure came another problem. Before dialysis she had to be given a laxative which caused her to have massive rectal bleeds, she then required blood transfusions and colonoscopies. She had diverticular disease which had haemorrhaged under pressure! One thing I hope came out of her suffering, the staff treating her learnt to be more cautious in the future with other patients, maybe she saved someone else from suffering? What happened was traumatic for her. She never recovered and in 2009 died in hospital six weeks after admission. We were not there at the time, we had booked a holiday and after much soul searching went ahead with the plan. Heather's sister agreed she would be with her when we were away.

We arrived home the day before the funeral. The journey over was not without incident. Our car decided to quit just as we reach Sawley and K's fiancé (she had got engaged whilst we were away) had to bring another car and we arrived an hour later than planned but still in time. Some weeks on, Heather noticed a mark on our bedroom window, on closer examination it was the outline of an owl, complete with wing feathers. She was convinced it was her mother's way of saying it was all okay.

Now Heather's dad was on his own, we always thought his health was worse and Hannah did a lot for him. He was very upset and lost without her, his condition deteriorated further, especially his mobility. He still managed to get a taxi on a Thursday night up to the Conservative club in Idle, sometimes we would drop him off. Eventually the taxi driver told him, out of kindness, he was not safe to go out. They would escort him up the drive and make sure he got in safely, then he would ring us to let us know he was back. We took him out for meals but as his movements became slower and stiffer, we couldn't get him in the car easily. We used to take him out in the wheelchair, he really enjoyed his outings. He used to like a gin and tonic when we went out, but that was stopped because we both tried to get him in the chair, but we couldn't without hurting him. It was too much for him, so we used to get fish and chips and he used to have his gin and tonic at home instead. We also had to make alterations to his care as he had an emergency call button put around his neck just in case he fell or had an accident. We arranged for carers, four times a day. This being Yorkshire, they gave him a cooked breakfast, bacon and egg, which he enjoyed. He'd been kept on a strict low-fat diet up to this point, but there comes a time when prevention has to give way to quality. Winston Churchill used to eat full English breakfast and drank whiskey and soda in the mornings and still lived to ninety years old, he died on the 24th of January 1965. So, we thought Heather's dad, Basil, a life-long conservative should be allowed to drink and eat as he wished. Then someone would come at lunch time to check to see if he was okay, providing him with a light lunch as at this stage, I do not think his appetite was great. Then someone came in the evening to provide him with a meal, and later on to get him changed and put him to bed with the TV on in his room. He did manage reasonably well for a while, but we noticed he was becoming quite frail. He had a few spectacular falls. One time, in 2012, we were in Montreal, Canada when Heather got a phone call. It was the Yorkshire police. Basil had fallen in the bathroom behind the door and the police had been called and had to break the bathroom window to rescue him. They had rung to ask us to arrange a glazier. We felt very helpless, Heather explained she was in Canada, so the police kindly got the window boarded. Basil was in hospital for about four weeks. We got to know all the social workers well during that time!

For me, I felt sad that we could not take him out as that was his highlight, but we tried to keep him comfortable and pain free, that was his wish. One Sunday, the carers asked us to come and to see him as an emergency because he was not feeling very well. His swallow reflex had given up and he was unable to eat or drink and choked if he tried which was distressing him. I thought he had a chest infection, so he was admitted to hospital. He survived five weeks, we visited every other day. Eventually he got a lovely side room and was comfy, sadly he never recovered.

This was the end of an era for the Hobson family, we had seen him that evening and said our goodbyes but as we were driving back home, he had passed away at about nine p.m. Heather arranged this funeral after discussion with her sister, after all she had arranged Hannah's. All went well as far as funerals go. I was satisfied we kept our promise and we looked after him in his own home until his last admission to hospital. That was his wish and we managed to follow it through. We had done so much driving during the last few years from Blackburn to Bradford and back, we had a very high mileage and we had to change our car, but it was all necessary and worth doing.

The house in Bradford was not well maintained and we had to put it up for sale, but first we had to empty it! Like many people of that generation, they had been hoarders and had a lot of stuff, including out of date jams, food, drinks. It was up to Heather and her sister to decide what they wanted to keep and what they wanted to get rid of. My job was to assist, and it was a very stressful time because I am not a patient person. I understood there was sentimental attachment for Heather, but it was so much stuff we had to go through. They had kept a lot of Heather's grandparents and aunt's possessions. There was a loft full of furniture, boxes, tools, clothes, photos and old records. They were both avid readers so there were hundreds of books, not to mention a sideboard, a mangle and washing machine and a lawnmower. Basil had set up a pulley, he'd sawn the sideboard in two, it was a feat of engineering and ingenuity! We have done many, many trips to the dump, charity shops, specialist collectors and also online sales. One day, I had a little argument with an officious man at our local waste disposal site. There were four or five others, but this one particular chap just took it upon himself to find fault. One time he complained we put a broken plate in the non-recyclable dumpster instead of in with the ceramics for which you needed a permit, at the time. So, we had to take the plate home and apply for a permit. Driving to Bradford continued, it took two years to clear and sell the house. In fact, we had people help us do it, and the house was finally cleared. We got the house ready and put it on the market, we had to reduce the price twice before it sold, and I got all the legal paperwork regarding the power-of-attorney and paid all the bills. Finally, what was left was divided between Heather and her sister and my job was done. After everything was finished, I felt saddened that I was not there to look after my parents, and I missed my father's passing, but I helped Heather's. God works in mysterious ways if you believe in God.

A New Nurse Joins Us and the Practice Continues
In 2000, our practice nurse was planning to retire. She had worked at Blackburn Royal Infirmary, but a few years before me. I think she was proper old-school, caring, kind and thorough with everything she did. When she joined our practice, she was coming back to nursing after taking a break to bring up her family. She needed some specific training, which she picked up quickly, she did not just practice nursing, but she helped me with minor surgery, sterilising and preparing the instruments the way I liked. Then she also learned to help me with my antenatal and postnatal clinics, she was one of the

192

best nurses I had worked with. She became part of an excellent practice team but sadly she was retiring as her husband had already retired. They had grandchildren and I think it was the best decision for her. I missed her help at the practice, but as they say, as one door closes another door opens.

Heather, was working part-time as a practice nurse in another single-handed practice and she got on well there. I discussed our nurse's retirement with my partner, and he suggested asking Heather, we both knew she was able to just step into the job. I was concerned about the staff feeling resentful working with the boss's wife. I knew some of them were a little apprehensive, but Heather really tried hard to fit in and in fact she easily became part of the team. If there was anything they were concerned or wanted to do differently they would even tell her to tell me. Professionally she was excellent, listening to peoples' concerns and she would pass this on to me and if she could go the extra mile to help anyone, she would. Her clinical knowledge was well above the nursing standard and many a time she used to argue with me about clinical matters, but she also knew I had to make a decision and it's not always easy with some patients. She certainly integrated into the practice well.

We still had an open surgery, and most patients had the 'in-house' investigations on the same day as we had a full-time healthcare assistant. She arrived not long after Heather and was trained in the surgery. She was really good at her job, as soon as I sent patients to her, she was quick to do the required investigations and many times I pushed her to her limits, but she never complained. I appreciated it but sometimes life is cruel, and she developed mesothelioma, an asbestos related cancer and passed away within two years of diagnosis. I was very sad, as were all the practice team. She was not only a good worker but a good person too and it was very hard for us all, and she was like one of your family.

As The Nature of The Beast Changes, So Do I!

Work continued as usual but there were a lot of changes. In light of Dr Shipman, the monitoring of doctors became more stringent, and revalidation was brought in. You had to attend a certain number of updates and courses to get your required points for the revalidation. Then another GP would come and discuss this all with you. I absolutely hated this because it was unnecessary and I saw very little benefit to it, it wouldn't catch a serial killer and it was easy for under-performing doctors to "blag". If I wanted to learn something I made an effort, paid from my own pocket and went to courses or meetings in my own time. I didn't want to leave the practice for no benefit. Most of my revalidation was done by people who were junior to me and with all due respect, I knew it was a paper exercise, but they did it as a job and got paid for it. This was putting a lot of doctors close to retirement off, I think! That's my personal view. I am not sure why, but when things are running smoothly some politicians always want to implement change things without any proof of benefit. My feelings were if you are a conscientious person and want to be the best doctor, you will do everything possible to improve your knowledge for the benefit of your patients. I had never had a problem attending any educational meetings where I am likely to learn and gain new knowledge, even if it means I have to pay for it.

During my time as a general practitioner in Blackburn, the secretary of state of the United States of America came to Ewood Park in Blackburn at the invitation of the Foreign

Secretary of the United Kingdom. This was around 2003, during the Iraq war crisis and there were a lot of protests against the war, at that time. I liked Tony Blair and his government, there is no secret about that, and I still do, but one of the mistakes he made was the Iraq war. A lot of people were against it, including Labour voters. Before the Iraq war, I wrote to Tony Blair, and I said if you are going to war in Iraq, which I do not agree with, can you at least create a democracy like ours in the UK?

It is fair to say that the UK democracy was one of the best democracies in the world at the time. I am not sure at present our democracy is functioning as it should. I will write more about the value of democracy later. We all know it was a bad judgement and created more problems in the Middle East than it cured. I did get a reply from Ben Bradshaw, at least signed by him in his capacity as the Parliamentary Under-Secretary for Foreign and Commonwealth Affairs 2001–2002. However, I still think Tony Blair did a lot for Labour, but not everybody will agree, I can expect that. It was my personal opinion, and I am happy about it, but the arrival of the Secretary of State for America had created some problems for me as a doctor. Our Ewood surgery was just at one of the entrances to Ewood Park football ground and I had a surgery to run. Security was very tight and there were police everywhere. The entrance to Ewood was blocked but my patients still had to come for treatment. The reception staff were already in, but when I tried to drive to the surgery, a police officer stopped me. He told me due to security he was not allowed to let anybody in. I told him that I understood he was doing his job and I asked him to let me do mine and see my patients, some of them could be seriously ill. I showed him my GP identification, but still he kept arguing with me. I told him he could watch me go into surgery and coming out so that I am not a danger to the Secretary of State, but if he stopped me seeing my patients and something happened to one of them, he would be responsible! Then he agreed to let me get through, I understand they have to provide security but there has to be common sense. I am not suggesting doctors cannot be criminals, Shipman proved that, of course there are some who commit crimes. I finished my surgery and went out and thanked him for letting me do my work. When I left, I was on my way to see a child as an emergency. This particular child I had seen the evening before with the signs and symptoms of an infection, but I was not sure what was going on. I had been in two minds whether to admit him or observe him at home with some medications. The mother was quite sensible, and I explained to her to ring up if his condition got worse, she was quite happy with this. Although, she did not ring I was still concerned just in case, so I decided to visit and rang to tell her I would call on my way home, but I could not be sure when as the police were blocking the roads due to the Secretary of State's visit. I set off, went through a few road blocks and I was going towards Preston New Road. There were traffic lights but no road block, so I just drove to the traffic lights and as I was entering it switched to amber and I proceeded to go through but out of nowhere this police lady came behind me with sirens going off, indicating for me to stop. I stopped and got out of the car as I was requested. She told me I drove through the red light, but I knew I hadn't.

'My word against yours,' I said. 'I did not go through the red light, it was amber!'

She responded saying, 'Do not say anything more,

otherwise I will arrest you!'

Politely I tried to explain that I was a doctor going to see a sick child and pleaded for her to not stop me. I offered to fill out the forms and documents once I finished my visit but asked to see this child first as I did not know how ill he was. She refused to listen and continued to say do not speak otherwise it will go against you in court! She gave me some paperwork and asked me to go to the police station within so many days and hand it to the duty officer. I was quite shocked by her behaviour and yet again she was very young and been told to protect the Secretary of State. What she did not understand was I was doing my job and if she doesn't agree with my statement about the red-light situation, she could let me go and sort the paperwork after as she had seen my driving license. Anyway, I went to the patient's house and examined the child, he was still no better I think he had a chest infection, so I admitted him to hospital.

I rang a solicitor friend. I told him the full, honest story, he was quite shocked. He thought that the police officer had no leg to stand on. He told me not to give them my driving license or any paper work, just go to the police station and show them. He said he would let them know he was representing me and ask them not to take my license. He sorted it out. I did not have to go to court, I was not charged with any driving offences. I got a letter from the police superintendent to explain that I had not been charged and the matter was closed, but no apology. What I learnt from these two incidents is that in any job you do you need to use your common sense and that comes with experience. I know this, because when I was younger, I used to get angry about any injustice I saw but as the years go by I've learnt to handle things differently.

I already mentioned our open surgery, but it could be stressful at times because you don't know how many patients you are going to see in the surgery, but I did not want to change this system because it was best for the patients. The staff found it easier than trying to arrange appointments and argue with the patients when there were no slots available, we also didn't have to contend with non-attenders. We did a survey of what our patients wanted and 99% who answered said they preferred our system.

One evening, I had been very busy at surgery, not just because of the number of patients, there were a lot of complications and many needed investigations and referral. At the end of the surgery everybody was stressed and stretched to their limits, and I just managed to finish at about six thirty p.m. Then the receptionist came into my office and said she had an emergency visit for me. A mother was concerned about her child and wanted to speak to me. I was really tired, but I always said I would never refuse a visit to a child. In truth, I did not refuse anybody, even adults but sometimes I could speak to them on the phone and sort things out. This lady didn't normally ask for visits, so it was unusual. I rang and told her I would call on my way home. She asked me if I was sure, the receptionist had told her I had a very busy surgery. This shows this lady was also concerned about me. I said I would rather see the child and not worry. I went on my way home after signing all the prescriptions and paperwork. When I saw the child, something was very striking, he was screaming, not just crying, as if something is really hurting him. He was refusing food, drink and paracetamol. There was no diarrhoea or vomiting, his temperature was marginally raised, no neck stiffness, no photophobia and no rash. His throat was slightly red, ears were normal, but something was bothering me. This could be early signs of meningitis, he was irritable. Adults can tell you if they have a headache but children cannot and so they cry. Sometimes, that can be an early sign, but you cannot admit every child with symptoms of irritability, but my gut instinct told me he needed close observation and I cannot sit with him all night. I suppose I could have relied on the parents, but I decided to admit him. I knew the on-call registrar would probably ask the questions about meningitis and why I wanted him admitted when there are no clear signs of meningitis. I rang and before he even started asking any questions, I told him there are no clear-cut signs of meningitis but there was something about his cry, irritability and refusing to take liquids and paracetamol and I said he needed close observation for at least twenty-four hours. If he was well after that, send him home and I would hold my hand up and say I was wrong. He argued how this admission was unnecessary. Then I said to him, I have worked in hospital, and I have been working long enough in general practice and I feel he needs admission and if you do not accept him, I will speak to the consultant, and I can assure you the consultant will accept this admission. I knew the consultant understood how difficult it can be to diagnose meningitis and I was sure he would accept the admission without hesitation. The registrar reluctantly accepted the admission and over the next twenty-four hours the child did not settle, his temperature rocketed, and he was put on a drip and given a lumbar puncture, which suggested it was bacterial meningitis. He was treated successfully with minimal complications. His mother had heard all my discussion with the registrar on the phone, later she came to surgery and thanked me for saving her son's life. I said it was just my gut feeling, I could not, not admit him. I wrote this because medicine is not black-and-white and sometimes patients do not present with the textbook picture. With experience you learn, in my whole life I have seen five meningitis cases and all of them presented slightly differently.

Another day a lady came to see me, probably for the first time, as she was the senior partner's patient and she liked him, so she always saw him. She seemed to have had irritable bowel syndrome and for a number of years he prescribed her medications for this. She managed well by all accounts, this time she had come for her repeat prescription, which she had not had for three months. She said her symptoms had got worse, hence the trip to surgery. My partner was away so she saw me, the receptionist explained she needed to be seen by a doctor because she has not had a prescription for a while. At first, she was hesitant because she had never seen me before which is quite natural. I said hello and made her comfortable.

I said, 'Can I ask you few questions if it's okay with you before I give you, your prescription?'

She said that was fine and I asked her, 'How often do you open your bowels?'

She replied, 'Six times a day and it was loose.'

My next question was, 'Has anything changed recently?'

'Oh yes,' she said. 'It's got a little worse.'

I think she was worried, she knew things were not right. After I finished taking a history, I asked if it was all right if I examined her. I just want to make sure everything was okay, she was a little reluctant and asked if it was necessary? I explained that in my view it was, but if she did not want to be examined that was her choice. I reassured her I would call my health care assistant to chaperone. I never examined a female patient without a chaperone. If there was a complaint, it was your word against the patient's and it could be difficult to defend, even with help from the Defence Union. Anyway, she agreed, and when I examined the left side of the colon, the descending colon felt thickened to palpation. This was the clinical impression, I have had lot of surgical experience and that was an advantage. I explained this to her and suggested a referral for a barium contrast X-ray for her bowel. Again, she was not happy, but I managed to persuade her, and she had the X-ray quite quickly and it suggested bowel cancer. I referred her urgently and after a colonoscopy and biopsy the diagnosis was confirmed. I saw her again and explained although she had bowel cancer, her other scans did not show any sign of spread and hopefully after the operation she should be fine. I added the point that she is unlikely to require a permanent colostomy as it was higher in the colon. She had surgery and all went well, and she had no further problems until I retired. They had moved ten miles away from Blackburn but wanted to stay with our practice if it was possible till I retired. I was pleased she did well. Doctors never stop learning and I am still learning even in retirement.

One of the things I did not like is people wasting NHS money. One day, one of my receptionists came into my consulting room and told me, a male nurse, employed by the CCG, Clinical Commissioning Group, wanted to make an appointment to see me. He wanted to discuss why so many of our patients were going to the accident and emergency department rather than to the GPs surgery. I could not really refuse, although I knew he was wasting his time because we ran the open surgery six days a week. No appointments needed, therefore, they did not need to go to accident and emergency. I said yes and in due course, this nurse, and I assume his secretary, came to see me. He introduced himself and explained his role in trying to reduce the number of people going to accident and emergency. He wanted to find out why our patients are going to accident and emergency. I asked him how much he knew about our surgery and how it works, he said he did not know.

Then I said, 'Don't you think you should have found out before you came to see me?' It would've saved him and his colleague a journey and saved the taxpayer money. He was quite taken back by my reply, I explained to him that ours was an open surgery, six days a week, no appointments needed. Although, there is an appointment system at our Larkhill surgery, those patients can come down to Ewood if they need to.

He said, "then why are they still going to hospital?"

I said, "the best thing you could do is send a questionnaire and ask them why they're going to accident and emergency department rather than going to GP surgeries."

I suggested they ask the reception staff in the A&E to hand it out to patients before they were seen. I told him that would give him the answers he was looking for. I pointed out he was a registered nurse, and his skills would be better placed in a clinical area rather than this. I said this was a waste of tax payers' money. He left quite quickly after that, and I do not think I totally blame him for this, it was the CCG who should have thought it through. I know he was given job to do and maybe I was too harsh but that's how I felt at the time.

The other day I was talking to one of our friends on the phone, because the Coronavirus lockdown means we were unable to meet up. We used to go out at least once a week for a drink, before that, when I was working, I used to see him and other friends after my evening surgery at our local pub. While we were talking, I remembered something and felt like writing about it, because it was quite interesting.

One evening after surgery, I went for a pint at my local and I met a few regulars.

One of them said, 'Shivaji, can I ask you a question? Although you must be tired after your evening surgery.'

I replied, 'Let me have sip of my beer and I will be ready.'

He told me he had been to see his own doctor with pain in both his legs, one side worse than the other. His doctor told him it was due to the tablets he was taking for his cholesterol. H said he just wanted my second opinion. He was taking statins to lower his cholesterol and they can cause muscle pain. Why statins cause muscle pain is not fully understood but there are two possible explanations. One theory is that the statins may affect the protein in the muscle cells which decreases the muscle growth. Another theory is that statins decrease the level of a natural substance in your body called co-enzyme Q10. This substance helps your muscles produce energy.

Anyway, I listened about his story, I knew he was diabetic and had heart disease. My brain went into action quite quickly and I asked him where and when did he get this pain, and he was very specific. The pain was in the calf muscles, and he got it when he walked and the pain went away when he rested, he did not get pain at rest. Red warning lights started to come on in my mind, he might have intermittent claudication? He was a perfect candidate as far as his history was concerned. He was diabetic with high cholesterol and heart disease, well I didn't ask him any more questions. I told him I do not want to spoil his drink, but it sounded like intermittent claudication. I explained what that meant, it was like angina in the legs. When you have high cholesterol, it sometimes deposits in the lining of the arteries supplying the legs as well as coronary and the neck arteries called the internal carotid arteries which can cause a stroke. When the artery narrows, sometimes bits of the cholesterol plaque break off and get into the circulation and the wall of the artery becomes irregular and impairs the smooth flow of blood. As the disease develops a type of blood cell called platelets sticks to the wall and forms clots. These clots can break off and travel along neck arteries towards the brain.

Exercise increases the oxygen consumption allowing muscles to contract and function properly. When there is a blockage in an artery, the lack of the oxygen leads to pain which is only relieved by rest. You do not need as much oxygen therefore you are pain-free. I said to him I'd pick him up the next morning, and drive to an old road I normally walk on as there are no cars allowed just walkers and cyclists. We drove to the place, and he began walking, then he could tell me when he got the pain, and I could record the distance. It was about two hundred yards on the flat road and would almost certainly be less on a hill. One leg was a little better than the other and he went three hundred yards. When he stopped walking within minutes the pain stopped, it was classic intermittent claudication, blocked arteries in both legs and one was worse than the other. I recorded all this on my phone and texted all the information to him including the history and claudication distance on both sides. I asked him to make an appointment with his GP. I had given him the information he needed, also at the end of my text I put my qualifications, MBBS, FRCS, RCPS. The reason for all this was it's nothing to do with me showing off, it's just to make the GP aware I am a qualified surgeon and I know what I'm talking about, although all doctors should know this. I've seen a few times cases like this in my surgical career. As I said, during my time we did everything as general surgeons because there were not as many specialists. These cases were more common then and are now generally diagnosed sooner as people are going to doctors earlier. Anyway, he went to his GP and was referred to a specialist, had an ultrasound scan of the arteries and an angiogram, which showed the blockage on both sides. He had an operation to improve his circulation and can now walk without pain. I don't think I mentioned it to him, but he could have lost one or both of his legs if it had gone untreated. Intermittent claudication is a progressive disease, and he was diabetic as well which can be a lethal combination.

I have performed below knee amputations on this type of patient in the past. I think some mistakes in medicine are made not because of lack of knowledge but because the person is not following a proper procedure of history taking, examination without shortcuts and most importantly listening to patients and I am very sad that it still happens quite often.

Retirement Looms
The practice was still doing well with no major issues, but my senior partner decided to retire and enjoy his life, and why not, he had every right as he had given his best to his patients and NHS. He was a good doctor, well-liked by all his patients and he was a generous host, always organising parties at his house with a wide variety of friends. I cannot blame him for retiring but it was not just a patient's loss, it was going to be hard to replace him and subsequently this proved correct. We had worked together for twenty-three years and never had a fall out. Yes, of course sometimes we disagreed but we also always knew how to compromise, and we both got along well. One day he said to our practice manager, Shivaji is the brainy one in the practice; that is the best compliment anyone had given to me. General practice partnership is like a marriage, you are working together day in, day out, and sometimes there are

bound to be differences of opinion, but you need to work to resolve them, and we did. We gave him a good send off, with several retirement parties, everyone was upset but we wished him well. Many patients came to the practice to see him before he left.

With his leaving I had to look for a new partner, so I put out an advert and I had three applications. Subsequently I interviewed them with my practice manager. The one that I chose to be my junior partner was an Indian doctor and he spent a lot of time working in paediatrics and had come late in life into general practice. His reference was from my colleague who worked with me as a house officer and had done well for himself. He had become a GP trainer. His reference was good and therefore I chose this doctor, although he was in his fifties. I decided from day one, I wanted to treat him like I was treated by my senior partner. I did everything I could to make him feel like part of the team. I arranged a similar contract that my partner had given me, three years parity and full partnership after that. In fact, I let him buy half of the practice premises and transferred my partner's patients onto his name to make him feel more secure in the practice, sadly in retrospect this was a mistake. It seemed to work well for the first couple years and then he got his full parity. I am not saying that's when things started to go wrong but there was something not quite right. There were a few little things, he wanted more time off and to make all the surgeries appointment only. He dithered and was insecure and declined to make decisions and requested people come back and see me, which was not good for the patients. Then we started to argue, a barrier came up between us. We took a third salaried partner with the idea that he will replace me when I retired but things were not going well between us. I tried to arrange meetings and discuss things, but it did not really help. He also preferred not to do open surgery. I think our personalities were different and I realised it was going to be difficult. When partners do not get on well, staff take sides and it just makes it worse for the whole practice and consequently, work suffers.

It is one of those things that started to go from bad to worse and it was when I decided to reduce my hours to become part time, but then he had started to argue about the profit share and holidays and the workload. I was disappointed to say the least. I had a choice as senior partner, either split the practice, ask him to leave or I leave, because the working conditions were causing stress and the patients might start to suffer. The patients also noticed when something was not right, because it created an atmosphere. In the end I decided to retire as I did not want to go through the trauma of a practice split up and legal issues. I had worked twenty-three years with my previous partner and many years in hospital, in total I had worked about forty years in the NHS, I was not used to this sort of situation. The salaried partner also sided with him, hoping I would leave sooner, and he would get my job!

I was very sad to leave on these terms as I had built up this practice with my senior partner and our practice was one of the best practices in the area. Finally, I took retirement, I refused a party and left on my birthday in 2013.

Heather was still working at the practice, but she found things had changed and used to come home stressed. Eventually, she retired, much earlier than she would have liked. She is younger than me and had a few more years of nursing in front of her. We were both now retired and, although we could've given a few more years to the NHS, that was the end of that for both of us.

I do not think many people realise a GP partnership is like

a marriage, if two partners don't get on for whatever reason it may be, it becomes extremely difficult to work together and a split up is like a bad divorce and can become acrimonious. Sometimes you have to go through solicitors, especially if partners do not want to resolve issues amicably. Having worked forty years in the Health Service, I did not want to go through the legal route, and I knew there was not going to be a compromise because this particular partner was hell bent on causing problems, I say this not out of malice, but I was proved right.

Just a few years after my retirement this partnership split. For whatever reason, the junior partner left suddenly, under a cloud and moved to Australia. Another partner came into the practice. Things did not work out with her either, it became so bad that—I was told by several sources—it went to the General Medical Council. Each partner blaming the other and writing complaints about each other.

Eventually the practice was taken over by another practice in the area and I think the Clinical Commissioning Group was involved in this. This was not a private matter anymore, a number of my patients told me what had happened, and it was public knowledge.

Retired but Not Out to Grass!

The day I left my own practice, it was very emotional for me and my staff who have been so loyal and helpful to me over the years, we became like a family. Tears were shed, for them too, it was a big change. I shed some tears also. They won't be working with me again and we had developed this bond and it was not just that we had become friends. After retirement, we still speak occasionally and go out for meals whenever we can. By the time the practice was taken over by another practice, very few of my original staff remained. As far as the practice is concerned after a few years, new partners and existing partners did not get on well and it was obviously not a happy atmosphere for the staff. Most of the staff worked with me either retired or joined another practice. It was end of the practice as we knew it, it was very sad to see everything we had built up destroyed.

After my senior partner's retirement, he did not live long enough to enjoy life and see his grandchildren as he died within a few years of retirement. I was very sad for him and his family.

In 2018, I was invited by one of my ex-patients for a charity dinner. They raised thousands of pounds for a cancer support charity in memory of a family member. On the table next to us was one of my ex-patients and towards the end she came and said we know why you left and look what happened to the practice. It's so sad, I must say I personally never discussed any personal problems with my patients but after my sudden departure the patients found out, somehow or other.

Initially I found retirement very hard because I went from being a busy GP to doing no work and still feeling the turmoil of emotion that leaving the practice left me with. I was still asking myself questions, should I have retired? Could I have done anything else? I decided to do GP locum sessions. I was approached by our friends who had their own practice. They were very willing to offer me sessions or a salaried position possibly because they knew how I worked. I decided to just do locum work whenever they needed me because I didn't want to take a regular job, in case things did not work out, my friendship would be damaged forever, and we have been friends for nearly forty years.

I started doing locums but it's not the same feeling of

satisfaction because you did not get to follow up your patients. Maybe I had not recovered from what had happened yet. Then another doctor approached me to do some locum work, now a number of GPs knew I had retired.

There is always in need for locums, especially if you are a single-handed GP. This particular doctor ran a single-handed practice in a village with only a small patient list size. It was a well organised practice, and he was very well liked by his patients and staff. He was from north India I think, probably a similar age to myself. When I met him to discuss doing a few locum sessions he was a pleasant and likeable man.

So, I decided to do work for him whenever he needed me. I started with one week at first then as time went by, he started to ask me to do more. One time he took a long break of about five weeks, I guess he trusted me to run the practice on my own. I started to like the practice, as the patients started to get to know me and developed a good working relationship.

The staff were very good, and they knew the job well, I even took them out for a Christmas lunch. This GP was thinking to retire, and I gave some thought about buying this practice, it was small and ideal for me but after a discussion with Heather we decided to just enjoy our retirement. I had already worked 40 years in the health service and given my best. I believe this practice was taken over by a group practice and that was it, I stopped doing locum work altogether.

The Family Flourishes
Now both of our children had grown up and finished their respective schools and blessed with good grades. Karina decided to do a drama degree at Manchester University. I did not know what her plan was, I did not influence our children regarding their career choice. It was their decision and I left it

to them to decide what they wanted to do. Karina graduated with a degree in drama, then she went to UCLAN in Preston to get further qualifications. She qualified as a broadcast journalist and used to work for the BBC in York reporting the news. Then she went on to do freelance journalism and read the news at various radio stations in the local area. She worked for ITV also but her career as a journalist stopped and she went into hospitality.

In August 2016 she opened her own very successful restaurant, Menagerie in Manchester. In 2015 she won an award for being the best young entrepreneur woman of the year in the north-west. She is now very happy with partner Ben and young son Henry. He is an absolute delight to us all, of course I am biased, but I do think he is the most beautiful baby.

In 2021 they became parents to a beautiful baby girl called Lily Eleanor. She is a little treasure, but again I am biased.

Sam went to Newcastle University and got a first-class degree in history, then decided to convert to law. He completed his training, one year in London then the final year in Manchester. He is now a fully qualified solicitor specialising in banking and he is working in Manchester and recently got married to Helen.

Cats and Dogs

Heather has always been an animal lover and back when we first met, she had taken on a disabled kitten, Kizzy. She had a deformed front paw, but it never stopped her. She had gone missing during our time in Liverpool and we had got two more rescue cats, then she reappeared! Sadly, one of the new kittens got knocked down but the other, Usha lived for fourteen years. Next came Tinkerbelle, Karina chose the name! Sadly, she had cat flu as a kitten and by five years old had epileptic fits and went blind and was too poorly to survive. Before our children went to university, they got two cats just in case we missed them. However, they did not ask whether we wanted them! So, we ended up with two cats. Lily, was Sam's cat and Mimi was Karina's. Surprisingly there was lot of similarity, Lily was very laid back and quite like Sam, but on the other hand Mimi was very much like Karina, very active and outgoing. One day Mimi went out in the garden, and we were out but when we came back, we could not find her. We looked but there were no signs, so we dropped leaflets all over our area but no news. Eventually after four weeks we decided she was gone for good; that was when we got the call from a local vet. She had been found, her micro-chip saved her! He said she has been injured, possibly due to attack by another cat or a dog or even a fox? She was limping badly, there was nerve damage to her front paw called brachial nerve palsy. The brachial nerve is actually a group of nerves in the armpit in humans. We were pleased she'd been found, but at the same time apprehensive about the future, but she managed well with her disability. She limped about on three legs and the sore on her injured paw healed eventually, although it came back now and then. On another occasion Lily went out only for short time but she did not come back. Yet again we searched everywhere, two weeks later we got a call from our usual vet, she had been found in Copster Green. We were away in Ravenscar and our kind friend went and collected her! They traced Lily because of her chip. I could not believe how thin she was, I think she had been chased by another cat and lost her direction and ended in the fields near where we live. She was found by a lady about three kilometres from our house, I know this because I sometimes walk down there. We had two problems with her, she was almost skeleton having lost lots of weight and she had lots of ticks everywhere. Despite all my medical training I had never learnt to remove ticks! We had taken her back to vets and got the ticks removed. Poor Lily, despite all our efforts she never regained her weight or mental state. She was traumatised and used to be terrified of even the slightest noise or movement of people. She had lost interest in life, sadly her condition gradually deteriorated, and no one could help her including the vet. We kept her as comfortable as we could, but she passed away. It upset us all very much because she was part of the family and that is why when we get animals, we have to think how emotional it can be. With each pet we vowed, no more animals.

Karina has two dogs, fawn pugs and just had a beautiful baby Henry. They live in Manchester, in a flat until recently and it is difficult for her to look after two dogs. Mungo, the youngest, is very active so we have them for the time being until she and her partner, Ben, move to a house.

Four legged dogs, a three-legged cat and two-legged baby Henry, what can go wrong? When Henry comes to visit us, it's like comedy, Henry likes to eat his snacks not sitting down at one place but crawling around while eating and the dogs follow him, they know he will drop some food and invariably he does. Mimi the cat used to stand her ground and sit in middle of all this mayhem. Heather and I are chasing Henry to avoid him having an accident but, by the end of the day we are so exhausted it takes a few days to recover. It's all good fun though!

I thought I would write a little information about ticks and one of the diseases they can carry, Lyme Disease. Ticks usually bite on the legs or feet when walking in long grass. After an infected bite, a red circular rash can develop. The rash can develop up to three months after being bitten and usually lasts for several weeks, but most rashes appear within four weeks. The rash is described as being like a bull's eye on a dart board, not everyone gets the rash though. Some people have flu-like symptoms, such as a high temperature, headache, muscle and joint pains, tiredness and loss of energy. Most tick bites are harmless, only a small number of ticks are infected with the bacteria Borrelia burgdoferi and Borrielia mayonii which cause the infection. A tick bite can only cause Lyme disease in humans if the tick has already bitten an infected animal. It is important to remove the tick as soon as possible, just in case. To remove ticks, you can use fine-tipped tweezers or a special tick-removing tool. Grasp the tick as close to the skin as possible and slowly pull upwards, taking care not to squeeze or crush the tick. Clean the site with soap and water or antiseptic, currently we have plenty of antiseptic wipes because of Covid-19. You need to be diagnosed by a doctor and treated with antibiotics only if you develop symptoms as described earlier.

You would think we would have learned from this experience, and we would not lose a cat again, but animals are like children, they always surprise you!

One day we had a delivery of our new greenhouse, and we were showing the van driver where to put the parts. We left front door open, the driver got all the stuff in the garage and said goodbye and left. Later, Heather was looking for Mimi, but could not find her anywhere. We were puzzled, she was getting older and never went far but she just vanished. Heather decided to ring the greenhouse company just in case she had gone in the van but by this time van driver had been to Manchester to deliver another greenhouse. Later they rang back, she had hitched a lift in back of the van to the headquarters in Stoke on Trent. They said they thought her leg was broken and she was disabled, well we knew it was Mimi. They kept her safe overnight and we picked her up the following morning, she had good short break, but we had a two-hundred-mile round trip.

The Battle between a Man and a Cat:
September 2020 — at present we have four animals in our house, the two pugs, Louis and Mungo, we had them for eighteen months as Karina and Ben are living in a flat. They are old boys now. Louis is deaf and Mungo does cause trouble on occasion! Sam and Helen have two cats, Nutmeg and Pepper, and now Mimi has passed away they can come and stay whilst Sam and Helen, go on holiday. They didn't like the cattery, it made them sick! The problem with his cats, are they are very fast, and we dare not let them out in case they run away. This was a challenge to us as we have to let the dogs out regularly. We developed a routine, I feed the dogs at six a.m. and let them out, then they snooze on the bed until we get up properly. The routine was monitored carefully by Pepper and Nutmeg and one morning Pepper decided to play a trick on me. She hid under the dining table, watching the morning events. As usual I fed the dogs and let them out. Fortunately, I checked to see if anyone was hiding, and I found her and managed to catch her and lock her away while the dogs went out. I am really grateful to our competent government, otherwise known as Cummings and Goings! They told us to be alert, in case COVID-19 walked in through our patio door.

This cat, Pepper is so fast like a moon shot, like our government says. This battle did not end here. I finished the morning breakfast routine and went upstairs back to bed, but Pepper decided to take revenge and started jumping on me and running away! She did this several times but when she ran out I managed to close the door, at least I did not have to have an eye test to spot the cat. This world beating episode saved me a trip to Barnard castle. I was pleased I won the battle against Pepper.

Holiday Memories

We always tried to have two holidays a year, and it was important we did because when you are doing a stressful job it is essential that you take a break and recharge your batteries. There is always something to look forward to and our favourite destination has been in the Caribbean. Heather and I went on our first Caribbean holiday as a married couple to Antigua. It was really special as Heather was five months pregnant at the time. We stayed in a little cottage about ten metres from the beach. There were mango tree branches hanging over the cottage and when the mangos fell, we could hear them thump and roll down the roof. The whole atmosphere was relaxing, and we met some lovely people. There was a post lady and her husband, a bank manager and his wife and a single lady from Bolton who came every year to sample the delights of the Caribbean. She always bought him little gifts! There was an American couple as well. This couple were very interesting, he was a marine biologist working for the American Navy. He told us some fascinating tales of experiments to train marine mammals to carry out certain underwater tasks. He also spoke about submarines and how they were working on making them invisible to sonar, etc. He chatted quite a bit about what the Americans were doing in the North Sea. His partner was a hand model in New York, she had very long, slender fingers. She also modelled for the covers of Mills and Boon romance novels. She stayed constantly in the shade as she needed to keep her skin milky white. Years later we saw him on TV talking about USA marine defence. One day we shared a taxi with them to see the island, we went to Shirley Heights and English Harbour; Antigua is a small island, and it was easy to drive around in one day. When we were leaving, we exchanged our addresses to visit each other but we never met again, but the memories are still there.

While in Antigua, there are two other memories I have. Heather does not normally go very deep in the sea, maybe up to her knees, nothing more. There was the clear blue Caribbean Sea and I absolutely love sea swimming. One day, I was swimming and Heather had ventured into just about ankle-deep water although we disagree about this! Heather thinks it was thigh deep and there was a band of thick weed and she felt something move under her feet and I heard this loud scream and I looked back to see who it was, and it was Heather whimpering, 'Get me out of here!'

I thought it was a shark or something so I swam back as fast as I could. I did not see anything apart from some slippery seaweed. I picked her up and took her to shore. There was absolutely nothing except weed because the water was so clear and that's a memory I will not forget. The second involved water skiing. Most people managed to water ski well, but I wasn't getting it right and I wanted to learn. I was quite sporty as a child and in medical school and I don't like failing, so I booked private water skiing lessons. I used to stand up, but I could not last long enough to getting going properly, I kept falling. I tried and tried but I just couldn't, it was embarrassing. I asked this guy, Frenchie to take me to a private beach so I could practice unobserved, but I could not get my act together and to this day I never managed. In 2016 we returned to the same hotel and Frenchie was still there selling boat rides! My daughter Karina learned in Barbados when we were on holiday, she was so quick and did not take long at all. That's one of my failures, I still do not understand why but I might try again one day.

Our family favourite destination was Disneyland in Florida, we either stayed in Disney for two weeks or one week there and one week at the coast. For the children, it's like a dream and we stayed in several Disney resorts. It was convenient, you go on rides early when the queues are not so long. All the resorts have different themes and are special in their own right. My favourite was Disney's Animal Kingdom, where you can see wild animals grazing from your room. The other one I enjoyed was the Polynesian resort, it's just naturally beautiful and the food was good, but you have to book well in advance.

One of our family short breaks was to Centre Parcs. There were a number of advantages in taking short breaks, we did not have to take time off work and the children did not have to miss school. We used to book weekends and when the children finished school on Friday we'd set off and come back late Sunday evening. For me, I used to do morning surgery and my partner would cover me and this worked well for us. At Centre Parcs, there was something for everyone. We used to take our bikes, although, I do not think either of our children were keen bike riders. Then there was a swimming pool, with slides and water sports. In the evenings, when you are back at the chalet it was as if you were in a forest, and it was peaceful and quiet. We also used to do nature walks and there were restaurants if you wanted to go out. In 2000 we decided to take Karina and a few of her school friends to celebrate her fifteenth birthday. We went to Whinfell Forest Centre Parcs near Penrith, north of the Lake District. As you can imagine five teenage girls running around in Centre Parcs was a handful and we were responsible for them. To add to the stress, we picked them up early from school, with the parents' permission and took two cars. At this particular time, I had a little argument with the Westholme School headmistress because they were missing two hours on a Friday afternoon and she was concerned about this, missing school was not ideal in her eyes. I did understand her concerns, but we had discussed this with the parents and asked them to ring the school, which they had done. There was a lack of communication between class teachers and the headmistress and of course, she was irritated about all of this. She was off hand with me, and I reacted similarly in response and that did not help the situation. Eventually, she agreed to let us take the girls and they had a great time and we brought them back safely to their parents. On the Saturday night we arranged for them to go alone to a restaurant, we gave our card payment details and left them to it. At eleven thirty Heather was getting anxious. Various text messages had been flying back and forth and they assured us they were being sensible. It was about the time Coyote Ugly was out and judging by some of the photos the girls had been entertaining the bar! The itemised bill taught us a lesson. Fifteen-year-old girls are more like fifteen going on twenty-five! They'd passed for eighteen plus and several Jack Daniels had been consumed! It did turn out one was sick in a bush on the way back to the chalet and being attractive young girls, the boys followed! Enter 'Momzilla'! Heather, raincoat over nightie, torch in hand, stomped off into the night to round them up! Needless to say, the girls had the best time! Over the years, we managed to go to all the UK Centre Parcs. One year, we celebrated Heather's father's birthday there.

We have been many times to the Caribbean, and we thought we might try Indian Ocean Islands, especially the Maldives. Scientists believe these islands will not be there in the future, as sea levels rise. Anyway, we booked it as a final family holiday. As the children grew each family holiday had a bitter-sweet feel to it, it could be the last holiday we all take together, needless to say, that day has yet to come! It was a twelve-hour flight from Heathrow to the Maldives capital, Male, situated on the south-west of Sri Lanka, and south of the equator. When we landed, we were taken in a De Havilland Sea Otter sea-plane which takes off from the sea and lands on the sea. It is not a very long flight, and the captain was bare-foot and wore shorts. He did not fly too high, you could see all the atolls, and submerged volcano tops. We stayed at the Hilton resort, Rangali Island. The whole island was about a mile in diameter, we could walk around in twenty minutes. In the middle of this island, there were some palms and tall, old trees where a colony of large fruit bats lived. They were the size of a fox and would swoop over the pool like prehistoric beasts. It was a very peaceful, laid-back resort, there was a main hotel building, where all our meals were served. Once we were on the island, we did not need to wear shoes as it was just fine sand everywhere and beautiful clear sea. Our accommodation was situated by the edge of the sea and was surrounded by a lot of greenery, each chalet had its own strip of beach. The shower was outdoors in the back of the chalet with lots of foliage around. It was amazing, there was one restaurant under the sea, we booked it just to see because the tasting menu was mainly fish and our family was not really fish fans, Heather is vegetarian, and Karina does not eat fish at all, but it was the experience you had to go for. They provided alternatives so it was all good. One of the things about these small islands they are on average eleven feet and eleven inches above the sea level and if and when the sea rises, these islands may disappear underwater. I am glad we did this trip as it was a wonderful experience.

Another time, we went to Mauritius, situated in the Indian Ocean where there are beautiful beaches, and the island is full of natural beauty. There is a large Asian population, mainly Indian, and the food had an Indian influence. Each lunch there was a buffet style selection but there was European food as well. On this holiday, we met an interesting man from Manchester, who told us all about his life. His father was originally from Mauritius but went to England to work as a psychiatric nurse in Glasgow. He had an affair with a Scottish woman, she became pregnant, but the father never knew. The woman was already married with three children. In those days, a child with an Asian father was difficult to pass off as your own and he was given up for adoption. He was adopted by a vicar and his wife and brought up in a loving home with every opportunity. He went to Cambridge and did well for himself, then when he graduated, he became a comedian and made a living touring the northern comedy circuits. He had come to Mauritius to look for his biological father but, he said coming to Mauritius had opened his eyes. This young man was really well spoken and well mannered. After spending time in

Mauritius, he decided not to search for his father. He thought it could open up a whole Pandora's Box of emotions for his Mauritian family, none of which he wanted to be responsible for. Instead, he enjoyed his holiday, walked in the ocean and immersed himself in Mauritian culture, he was also a white witch which in itself was interesting. One evening he and his partner joined us for drinks and he said to Sam if he wanted to go to Cambridge or Oxford he needed to apply for the least popular subject and later on change it to the subject he wanted to study. Well, Sam of course did the opposite and applied to study for history at Oxford, one of the most popular subjects at the time. He went for an interview but did not get in, finally going to Newcastle, which suited his personality better. In a way, I am glad he went to Newcastle as he was very happy there and his mentor, a history lecturer was a wonderful lady. He was not stressed, it is my belief he would have been at Oxford, and he came out with the first in history at Newcastle.

In Mauritius we toured the island and visited a Hindu temple high up on a hill side but by a lake. It had rained and the lake had flooded the temple grounds and fish swam between the benches outside the temple. We saw spectacular waterfalls and other sites of outstanding beauty. The capital, Port Louis has a strong French influence, as the French inhabited this island as well as the British. The Indian population were brought here to work on plantations, and they settled. I am glad we took this trip and met some nice people like that young man from England on my life's journey. Again, this was a last family holiday!

Since our children had moved away and were getting on with their own lives, we decided to take a holiday to celebrate our thirtieth wedding anniversary in 2013. We booked to go to

Tobago, a small Caribbean island we had never been to. There are two islands paired together, Trinidad and Tobago. Trinidad, has many problems and is not on the regular tourist track but I had always wanted to go there. When we first went to the Bahamas, all the locals called me Trinni-Man, it seems there is a high number of Indians living there and I looked like one. We made the decision to go to Tobago because it was new to us and looked beautiful and the holiday resort looked natural and unspoilt. We were right, it was one of the lesser developed Caribbean Islands we have been to. The resort we were staying at was on the beach with a man-made lagoon pool. There was a special suite where Prince Charles stayed in, you can book it, but it was too expensive for us. Pavarotti had also stayed but that suite was cheaper! The pace of life was slow there, by ten p.m. the hotel was silent, and guests had turned in for the night. There were only a few other hotels on the island and there was a lot of natural forest. We toured the island and explored some of the rainforest. This is where we saw a large colony of leaf cutter ants, building a huge nest. The forest was unspoilt, my only regret was that we should've done a walking tour of the island, but it would have been too difficult for Heather. We did a catamaran cruise around the island, stopping to swim in Cotton Bay with a very large but friendly manta ray. At first, I thought it was a stingray! Heather just took pictures from the boat because she doesn't like swimming in the sea. It was a wonderful experience and some happy memories.

Life Goes On

One day, I went to my local post office to drop off a parcel when someone came up to me. I recognised her, she was one of my patients from Ewood. We started talking and she told me her mother, now in her nineties, always asked about me and that was very good of her I thought. Anyway, I enquired about her health, and she said she was doing fine except for her arthritis. I thought that was indeed very good, considering she had survived ovarian cancer many years ago.

This particular lady had come to my surgery with very vague symptoms of bloating, and she said something just did not feel right. There was no loss of weight, she had a good appetite but felt tired. I examined her abdomen and did an internal pelvic examination but could not feel anything abnormal. As a precaution I arranged some investigations, including the CA125 blood test. This is a marker for ovarian cancer and sadly it came back raised. Then the pelvic ultrasound scan suggested it could be ovarian cancer, both of these raised a very high probability of ovarian cancer. The problem for doctors and patients with a diagnosis of ovarian cancer, the symptoms are multiple and very vague, like indigestion, bloating, urinary frequency and changes in the bowel habits. So, it could be anything or just simple irritable bowel syndrome. The ovaries are situated deep in the pelvis making palpitation and internal examination difficult, therefore as a doctor you have to work on a high degree of suspicion. I referred her to a gynaecologist who confirmed it was what I suspected, and she was treated successfully. As it was detected early, she survived. When it hasn't been diagnosed early, it can spread locally or to other parts of the abdomen, liver, etc. Then the prognosis is not as good. There are three main types of ovarian cancers:

The most common is epithelial cancer arising from the lining of the ovaries.

The second one is stromal cancer, arising from the

structure of the ovary. The third type is rare and arises from germ cells.

It is difficult to diagnose which is why it is often not diagnosed early, patients do not go to the doctors because of the vague symptoms. This lady is one of the success stories and was still enjoying life in her nineties. These things remain deep in your memory.

What I learnt on my journey
I have noticed, even as a child as far as I can remember, whenever I got stressed my choice of treatment has been exercise. When I was younger, I used to run or go out on my bicycle or to the gym at college. When I got older, running was not really an option but I continued biking. However, nowadays, traffic worries me, and I decided to take on walking as my main exercise.

In 2016, I was stressed, I had retired early before I was ready and then Karina went through a stressful time, and I used to have restless nights. I decided to go back to exercise. I am not suggesting it works for everyone, but it worked for me. On the 11th of August 2016, I started walking every single day and I have continued up to date. Every day I write how far I have gone on my calendar. Initially, I walked around two kilometres a day, then I gradually, over a month, increased it to seven kilometres a day. Seven kilometres is just about ten thousand steps and since then, I have never missed ten thousand steps a day, even on holiday. Now I walk on average ten kilometres a day and a maximum eighteen kilometres. This exercise does not require special preparation, just good shoes and a coat. Walking is not like other forms of exercise such as biking or even running, if I cannot go out for any reason, I walk in the house, in the garden, anywhere I can. To date I have managed to do fifteen thousand kilometres and I am happy with it. I will continue as long as I can, but my family tell me I have been doing too much. Yes, sometimes I do feel tired, but if I keep walking thirty minutes at a time over a day, I can hit my target. Not everyone can do it or wants to spend that much time. I have met so many people on my various walks in the Ribble Valley and we have some good chats.

Earlier, I was saying I wanted to do things which I could not do before. I am very interested in history and wanted to know more about the formation of the NHS, how it started, who started it and how they got all the staff, nurses, doctors, carers and domestic staff and so on. I also wanted to look into how medicine in my own life time had changed, not just in the medical aspect but the new technology, I will be writing about this part of my journey next.

The Creation of the National Health Service

Aneurin Bevan was the man responsible for the creation of the National Health Service on the 5th of July 1945. The National Health Service, NHS, was the first universal health care system established anywhere in the world. A leaflet was sent to every household in June 1945 explaining that it would provide all the medical, dental and nursing care for everyone, rich or poor and any man or a woman or a child can use any part of it. There were no charges, except for a few special items. There were no insurance qualifications, but it was not a charity, people would have to contribute towards it. This would be funded mainly through a national insurance scheme and would be a relief to money worries in times of illness.

The Centre of Information for the Ministry of Health.
Dr Benjamin Moore, a Liverpool physician, in 1910 was probably the first one to use the words National Health Service. He established the state medical service association which held its first meeting in 1912 and continued to exist until it was replaced by the Social Service Association in 1930. Aneurin Bevan, the Minister of Health in 1945, was the main person in charge of creating the health service work force.

In 1955 the Ministry of Health had recruitment campaigns in sixteen British colonies.

By 1965, there were more than three thousand Jamaican nurses working in British hospitals, most overseas nurses were from the Caribbean, but some were from the Philippines and south Asia. Doctors were recruited from British colonies in particular India, Pakistan, Bangladesh and Sri Lanka.

In 1971, qualified overseas doctors constituted as thirty one percent of the workforce of doctors in the NHS. I did not realise this until I started to research the foundation of the NHS. I had been able to apply for a job in the UK through this recruitment drive created to fill the "skills gap" in the NHS. The NHS total work force, in 2017 was 1.87 million.

Aneurin Bevan, who had the vision to create such a wonderful institution should be very proud of himself, wherever he may be in his afterlife. He had to work hard to get all the consultants on board as they had lucrative private practices. Aneurin Bevan said he had to, "stuff gold in doctor's mouths", which was no easy task, but he managed. I have never seen a better free health service anywhere in the world.

In January 2020, the US spent more on health as a share of the economy and nearly twice as much as the average of countries such as the UK. Yet it has a lower life expectancy and the highest suicide rate among the eleven most developed nations. The US has the highest chronic disease burden and obesity rates, which is two times higher than the OECD— Organisation for Economic Cooperation and Development— average.

I have had personal experience of using the US healthcare in 1988 when we were on holiday in Florida. The NHS is cheaper and better for everyone, rich or poor, man, woman or child, as the founding father wrote in his first booklet. It has, not only treated millions of patients, but also helped train doctors from all over the world and in turn those doctors have helped millions of patients not just in this country but worldwide. My own medical college professors were trained in our NHS. No matter what, I would not swap the NHS for any other system in the world.

In my own career, the NHS helped me to get the necessary training I needed to become a surgeon, then a general practitioner and in return I treated and helped thousands of patients in my forty years of service. The patients trusted me and hopefully I have repaid the trust by helping with their needs. It was a mutual respect, and I am very grateful to the NHS for this.

In my time, every government has tried to change how the NHS is run, in various ways and I think, in my view, how the NHS was organised when it first started is still the best. It could be argued that there was less demand, less technology, science has progressed etc., so it had to change. I am not suggesting something is totally wrong with it now, although it is underfunded and parts are not functioning as they should, i.e., too early discharges, long waiting times for casualty and outpatients and the closure of smaller hospitals leading to the centralisation of services. Patients have to travel much further. For example, treatment of pyloric stenosis in infants was common in district hospitals in the '80s but now only performed at specialist units. The system was so well organised as a self-contained unit with consultants, senior registrar, registrar, senior house officer, junior house officers, matron, ward or theatre sister, staff and enrolled nurses, student and pupil nurses, auxiliary nurses (health care assistant), ward aid and dedicated cleaning staff. For every patient someone was responsible for their care and every member of the team knew their role, there was proper discipline and most importantly the patient benefited from it.

In my time, since I became a GP, I have written letters to most health ministers and almost all have replied. The ones I liked the most for the honest, straight forward replies I received were Alan Johnson and Kenneth Clark. I liked Alan Johnson and his work in various departments in parliament. I read, Johnson's books, "Please Mr Postman" and "This Boy". His book, "This Boy" won the Royal Society prize for literature in 2014.

When I qualified as a doctor in 1971-72, we did not have many investigations. This is not just in India but also in the UK. There were X-rays and some basic blood tests but nothing as advanced as today. We were taught to diagnose by history, symptoms and examination. This was drilled into us so well, if you do not get it right in the majority of cases you failed your examination. That stayed with me for the rest of my life, the only thing we were not taught well was neurology. It was not well developed at undergraduate level and was very basic, but I remedied this deficiency when I worked at Guy's and King's College Hospital. Therefore, as a GP I was able to do a good neurological examination and my neurological diagnostic skill was very good even though I say so myself. When I sent for investigations later on, my first impression was invariably accurate when the X-ray or scan confirmed it.

One day my GP colleague asked me how I could diagnose consolidation of the lung. On this particular patient, the X-ray findings were exactly as I had described, upper lobe of consolidation, this is seen in pneumonia. I was used to listening to breath sounds and could recognise these things, it surprised me other doctors couldn't! I think that part of examination may be dying, as investigations can do the same job but probably more accurately, I suppose.

The changes started to happen very quickly as the first advances came in investigation. The ultrasound scan was originally dated from a classic Lancet paper from Ian MacDonald and his team in Glasgow in 1958. However, there are medical papers as early as 1801, discussing the theoretical possibility of bouncing sound waves and capturing their image. It was used infrequently in the '60s but became more routine in the early '70s.

The ultrasound machine has a microphone, and it gives off sound waves which bounce off the organs inside the body and the microphone picks them up as "echoes". The microphone links to a computer which turns those sound waves into a picture on the screen. This technology is also called sonography, it is similar to that used for sonar and radar which helps the military to detect planes and ships. Ultrasound allows doctors to visualise problems with organs, blood vessels and tissues without having to make an incision. In my time, I remember if an examination and test did not help us make a diagnosis, we used to open the abdomen with quite a big incision, the procedure was called an exploratory laparotomy. This was a very invasive procedure, usually leaving a scar running down the centre of the abdomen, even if we still did not find anything the patient still needed to stay in hospital for at least a week. Ultrasounds do not use radiation, like an X-ray and for this reason it is the preferred method of viewing the developing foetus during pregnancy. In fact, this scan has become so advanced you can see the chambers of the heart in early pregnancy and many other major organs so that any abnormality is detected early, and in some cases, operated on before the baby is born. This is a major advance and ultrasound is one of the safest methods available. There are different types of ultrasound scans. The external scan, where a sonographer uses a probe on your skin. The internal scan, when a doctor or a sonographer inserts a probe into your body for example into the vagina to check the pelvis, uterus and ovaries, or the back passage to inspect the prostate gland, in men. There is another type called endoscopic scan, the doctor uses the flexible tube called an endoscope to look at the oesophagus, the tube that carries food from your pharynx to the stomach.

These advances in investigation, I had to get used to, and it has made a huge difference in early diagnosis and treatment of a variety of conditions including cancer but for me it was a totally new area.

A computerised tomography scan also known as a CT scan, is one of the more recent investigations but still it is a version of an X-ray. I am not particularly keen on this investigation as although it helps in the diagnosis, I am always concerned about the effects of radiation. Nonetheless, I will explain how it works and its advantages and then people can make their own judgements. This is an imaging procedure that uses computer processes and a combination of many actual measurements taken from different angles to produce tomographic image on virtual slides of a specific area of the scanned object. This allows the user to see inside objects without cutting into them. In 1979, the Nobel Prize for physiology and medicine was awarded jointly to South African-American physicist, Alan McCormack, and British electrical engineer, Godfrey N. Hounsfield for the development of computer assisted tomography. There are various types of CT scans, one of them is the position emission tomography or PET scan, another is the single proton emission computer tomography, SPECT X-ray tomography. CT scans produce data that can be manipulated in order to demonstrate various bodily structures based on their ability to absorb the X-ray beam. Today it is used widely on almost all parts of our body.

Magnetic Resonance imaging, also known as MRI, is a type of scan that uses strong magnetic fields and radio waves to produce detailed images of inside the body. An MRI scanner is a large tube that contains powerful magnets. The patient has to lie inside the tube during the scan and the MRI can be used to examine most parts of the body including the brain, spinal-cord, joints and blood vessels. The MRI scanner is operated by a radiographer, who is specially trained. You can talk to the radiographer through an intercom, and they can see you on a monitor throughout the procedure. The patient can use earplugs or headphones to reduce the noise of the loud tapping sound, this is the electric current flowing through the scanner as it alternates on and off. The procedure can last fifteen to fifty minutes, depending on which part of the body is being scanned. The MRI scan works because most of the human body is made up of water molecules which consist of hydrogen and oxygen atoms. At the centre of each hydrogen atom are even smaller particles called protons. Protons, like tiny magnets, have a north and south pole and are very sensitive to magnetic fields. When a patient lies under the powerful scanner magnets the protons in the body line up in the same direction, like iron filings when a magnet is run over them. Short bursts of radio waves are then sent to certain areas of the body knocking the protons out of alignment. When the radio waves are turned off the protons realign which is picked up by receivers in the machine. The signals provide information about the exact location of the protons in the body. These also help to distinguish between the various types of tissues in the body because protons are different in each tissue and realign at different speeds and produce different signals. In the same way that millions of pixels on a computer screen can create complex pictures, signals from the millions of protons in the body are combined to create a detailed image of the inside of your body. It is a safe investigation as there is no ionising radiation involved. It is very important diagnostic tool as in certain parts of the body like the brain and spine it gives you a detailed and accurate picture. Obviously not everybody can have this investigation as if there was metal inside the body, such as a joint replacement, pacemaker or any metal implants in the body, these strong magnets would attract the metal and it will be pulled towards the magnet. If you are claustrophobic, you may need anaesthetic or sedation, but yet again this advance in technology has improved diagnosis, especially in areas previously inaccessible, like the brain, and patients with Arnold Chiari malformation in the brain, it is a very important investigation.

There have been huge advances in cardiology too and in the early days of my career there were not many investigations other than ECG. We had to rely on clinical judgement and the ECG, the Electrocardiogram, which records electrical activity in the heart. Cardiac impulses start from the pacemaker area, a specialised tissue on the upper part of the right chamber of the heart called the sinoatrial or SA node. This electrical activity spreads to the whole of the heart in one particular manner and helps the heart muscle to contract and pump the blood. An

ECG can give valuable information in the case of myocardial infarctions, heart failure and abnormalities of the rhythm of the heart. Now there are many more investigations available. Dye can be injected into either an artery in the arm or groin and a catheter can be passed along the artery into the coronary artery and then an X-ray can show any blockage of the arteries, and this can then be either treated by a stent or a bypass.

We also now have defibrillators of various types:

External defibrillator, an automated external defibrillator or AED can be used in patients with ventricular fibrillation, a rapid ventricular heart rate, which can lead to cardiac arrest and death. If the heart stops, it is called asystole and in this case you cannot use this device. Nowadays, they can also be used to slow heart rates as well. They are placed in sport centres and shopping centres, etc.

People who have threatening cardiac arrhythmias, which are severely irregular heartbeats, can have a special type of defibrillator called an implantable cardioverter defibrillator, surgically placed inside the body to prevent sudden death. These pacemaker devices are fitted when the heart rhythm dysfunction is so severe and affecting your cardiac function and medications are not able to control it. This device is inserted under local anaesthetic into the upper chest just below the collarbone and a wire is passed into the vein and guided under X-ray scan control to one or two chambers of your heart and inserted into the wall of the heart chamber and attached to the pacemaker and this device will control your heart rate.

As for medication, the advances for heart disease means there are a lot more choices. Sometimes the older medications like digoxin are still used for heart failure, irregular heartbeat, or chronic atrial fibrillation. Now we also have drugs called

ACE inhibitors and other newer drugs for irregular heartbeat. One other drug we still use is furosemide, a diuretic to get rid of excess fluid. We have more medications to lower cholesterol called statins and this is a new addition in my time.

These advances have made so much difference, people are living longer and are more comfortable. I've seen someone recently in our area and she had quite a severe irregular heart beat called atrial fibrillation. This caused her heart to begin to fail, leaving her extremely short of breath and with swollen legs due to fluid retention. She was given an electric shock procedure called cardio-version and her heart returned to a normal rhythm and the medication got rid of her retained fluid and she felt almost normal. These are benefits of the medical advances I would never have imagined.

In surgery there have also been numerous advances. Now many operations are done through keyhole, laparoscopic or endoscopic surgery. Even surgery for bowel cancer can be performed laparoscopically, also a tumour can be removed from the lung through keyhole surgery. It reduces the stay in hospital as healing is much quicker and less painful and the results are very good.

There are numerous advances in medical treatment of multiple sclerosis, Parkinson's disease, arthritis, diabetes. When I started my GP practice there were no computers, all our prescriptions were hand-written. Acute prescriptions were written by the doctor and repeat prescriptions by the reception staff. This was a lot of work, and when computers first came into general practice, I was very reluctant to start using them, but I had no choice, either learn or get left behind. Our reception staff used to go on training courses, and of course we also had to, but if we had any difficulty, we had help. It was a slow process but eventually I had to go on more than one course and learn how to use a computer for consultations. Now, young doctors have no problems because they are learning computer skills from an early age. Certainly, this technology made a huge difference to the reception staff not having to write hundreds of prescriptions every day. Even now, I am not good at typing on computers although I get by.

Since I retired, there has been further advancement in GP surgeries and computing. Now there are GP apps, and we can order prescriptions online which are sent electronically to the pharmacy who then deliver them to your house. You don't even have to leave home. If you wish you can have a video consultation with your GP which is very interesting and useful at present because of Covid-19. One thing I still find difficult to understand is that we are losing the GP-patient contact. Of course, like anything else we have to get used to it. I do miss patient contact though, I can look back and wonder how far we've come and what is going to be next. I couldn't have imagined the changes that have happened in my lifetime, but they have. The new generations of doctors, will never know what it was like in the past, like when I used to watch Dr Finley's Casebook and think "How did he manage it?"

Cancer

As a doctor, if I did not write about this dreadful disease I will fail in my duty. There are about 14.1 million new cancer cases every year in the world and there are more than a hundred types of cancers, but modern treatments have improved the survival rate and it is lot better than it used to be. My experience of cancer is from what I have seen in my time as a working doctor and my general observations. Some types of cancer are almost cured. I have seen patients who have been disease-free for more than twenty years. I know of a man, a jump jockey and subsequently a well-known trainer, who had testicular cancer more than twenty years ago and, as far as I know, he is still disease-free. I've seen a colleague, who had testicular cancer which had spread to his brain but after treatment he has been disease-free at least for ten years. I remember two of my patients, one with rectal cancer and another with ovarian cancer and both disease-free for at least twenty years.

Why do people get cancer? The biological reason for cancer is, the body cells are dividing all the time and being replaced by new cells every minute of every single day. During this process if something goes wrong, for example the cells become damaged by the carcinogens in tobacco. Tobacco contains more than fifty known carcinogens, heavy metals and carbon monoxide. A lack of the right nutrients can contribute to cancer formation.

These newly damaged cells start to function differently and keep multiplying excessively. We call these cell mutations, and the body has a capacity to correct them but when overwhelmed with this rapid cell growth, these abnormal cells can keep growing and spread further into the body. This is called metastasis.

The body is wonderful machine and tries hard to correct any abnormalities but when you overload its capacity to deal with them, it cannot cope, and you develop the disease. There are numerous known factors which contribute to the development of cancers. As far as I am concerned nobody is immune to it, even if you do all the right things, but you can reduce your chances of getting it.

Skin cancer: As we speak skin cells, like other types of body cells are constantly dividing and new cells are formed. To function properly they need constant supply of appropriate materials, nutrients, vitamins and minerals in the diet. We also need to avoid anything which can cause cell damage in case the skin has excessive exposure to UV rays, sunlight, especially in fair skin people. What we can do to avoid excessive sunlight exposure? Primarily by protecting the skin using sun block to reduce the UV radiation and prevent burning the skin.

To help lessen the likelihood of many cancers, stopping smoking, reducing weight and exercising regularly and eating a healthy diet and fruit and vegetables are known to help. Going for screening when it is advised can also help protect you. At the time of writing there is routine: breast, cervix, bowel, prostate screening. Prostate screening is now advised for men over sixty.

Health, Disease and Wellbeing

BREATHING

Have you ever asked yourself one question? We pay for the water we drink, we pay for the food we eat, we pay for the clothes we wear but we do not pay for the oxygen we breathe. Why?

Oxygen, it can be argued is the most important constituent of the air we breathe, but we take it for granted. We breathe it in and out every minute of every hour, of every day but never think where does it come from? Without enough oxygen how long can you survive? The answer is no more than three minutes, but you can survive three days without water and three weeks without food.

By volume, air contains 21% oxygen, 78% nitrogen, 0.93% Argon and 0.04% carbon dioxide and a small amount of other gases. Air also contains variable amounts of water vapour, on average about 1% at sea level and 0.4% over the entire atmosphere. Humans consume five hundred and fifty litres of oxygen a day but where does all this oxygen come from? It comes from tiny ocean plants called phytoplankton that live near the surface of the ocean and drift with the current. All plants produce oxygen as a by-product of their respiration. They use the sun's energy, water and carbon dioxide to produce sugar for energy using the process of photosynthesis. Eight molecules of carbon dioxide (CO_2), eight molecules of water (H_2O) produce six molecules of sugar (CH_2O). There is a simple experiment which can be done in the garden. Put a leaf in a jar of water and leave in sunlight for a couple of hours and you will see tiny gas bubbles on the surface; that is oxygen.

The Amazon rainforest takes in one hundred billion tons of carbon and stores it, every year. The second largest carbon usage in the world is the Congo rainforest, in Africa. Therefore, when we breathe, we are using the oxygen produced by plants and the carbon dioxide in the atmosphere is taken up by plants and stored. Without this process life will not exist on Earth. That is why it is so important to believe in science and protect the planet. We have been more acutely aware of the importance of oxygen because of the coronavirus, COVID-19. Coronavirus deprives patients of this most important chemical, oxygen. When we breathe air goes into your lungs, in the lungs there are tiny sacs called alveoli. These alveoli are in very close contact with small blood vessels called capillaries, the oxygen in the alveoli is exchanged and transferred into these capillary blood vessels and carbon dioxide is transferred out and we breathe it out. Oxygen is transported by red blood cells from the capillaries into the larger blood vessels called the pulmonary veins to the left side of heart, then into the aorta and from there it is distributed all around the body, including vital organs like the brain, heart, liver, kidneys. These vital organs are each made up of millions of cells and each cell requires oxygen to metabolise the food we eat to produce energy. Without oxygen the cells cannot do this and depending on how many cells are deprived of oxygen, the organ fails to function at varying degrees. If all these vital organs fail, we call this multi-organ failure. So far scientists have published three theories as to how the coronavirus causes damage:

The first theory suggests the virus causes a severe inflammatory reaction in the region of the alveoli, it is described as pneumonia. However, it is not a true pneumonia which we would treat with antibiotics. It is thought that Covid-19 affects small capillaries in the lungs and interferes with the oxygen transfer at this level. If you look at an X-ray picture it has an appearance like broken glass, called ground glass appearance. This is treated by giving extra oxygen in various ways, depending on the severity. In severe cases, by ventilation, and less severe cases, by mask or nasal tubes.

In the second theory it is thought there is another mechanism by which Covid-19 interferes with oxygen transport. When oxygen enters into the blood it attaches to the haem part of the haemoglobin in the red blood cell. Haemoglobin is made up of globulin, a protein and haem, which is iron. This carries oxygen around the body, but according to this theory, Covid-19 attaches to the haem part and displaces the oxygen. The free iron is released into the blood and not only is oxygen not delivered to the vital organs, but the extra iron which is circulating freely is deposited into organs like the liver, causing dysfunction. Ideally, exchanging damaged blood through fresh blood transfusions should help, at least temporarily. This theory was published but I've not seen anything since so it may need more validation, but if it is true then it is an option for treatment.

The third theory that some scientists believe is that there is an increase in thrombosis in the lungs and the veins in the lungs. These small thrombi or clots can then be circulated to the various organs like the brain arteries, causing a stroke or blocking the arteries supplying blood to the heart, causing heart attacks. The anti-clotting drug, heparin, has been mentioned as a possible additional treatment but it is known fact that infections can increase clot formation and it is not yet known whether this is specific for Coronavirus. So far patients in the study were high risk, with underlying conditions such as high blood pressure and heart disease. It is still early days to be sure and we need bigger studies, to evaluate the findings.

As far treatments are concerned there are two which have been tried successfully: a drug called Dexamethasone has been used with some success in severe cases. Dexamethasone is a steroid and well tried and tested. It has been used since the 1960s, it has a powerful anti-inflammatory effect. Another drug called beta-interferon has been used in multiple sclerosis. Doctors at Southampton University Hospital believe if this drug is administered via a nebuliser, as a fine droplet aerosol directly into the lungs it can help. I think they have studied it in one hundred patients with success and are looking for a bigger trial at present. Recently, there has been a trial of antibody therapy, results pending.

October 2020 — there has been a report in the New England Journal of Medicine. Recovery Trial — this trial was carried out in the hospital setting on Covid-19 patients to establish the efficacy of dexamethasone. The study looked at patients with:

- Damage to the alveoli in the lungs
- Inflammatory Infiltrates
- Microvascular thrombosis

In these patients the inflammatory marker C-Reactive Protein was raised.

The conclusion of the study was patients fared better if treated with 6 mg dexamethasone daily for ten days but started seven days after they first displayed COVID-19 symptoms. Patients who were given mechanical ventilation benefitted most. This suggests Dexamethasone only works if there is inflammatory lung damage. That means starting treatment before lung damage has no benefit. In addition, it showed mechanical ventilation reduced mortality significantly. This again suggest it is the body's immune response that may be the cause of lung damage rather than the viral replication because steroids are powerful immunosuppressants.

Newspapers report Trump received dexamethasone on Friday the 2nd of October 2020, which means he must have had the disease at least seven days prior to that to have benefitted from dexamethasone and oxygen. The public never got the true story of when his symptoms started. He must have been spreading the virus for seven days prior to treatment, this seems to be a logical conclusion.

UK and USA have already updated their guidelines and it is now standard to receive dexamethasone in patients with lung damage along with oxygen. I believe Trump also received COVID antibody treatment, although the trial is not yet complete.

At the time of writing, there are more than one hundred trials going on for a COVID-19 vaccine, some are using genetic materials and others inactivated virus or part of the virus. In my view we will have Covid-19 vaccine by end of the year, so there is hope.

In general terms, to keep us in good health, breathing in clean, unpolluted air plays an important role. That is part of my argument about the environment.

Another point is to avoid anything which causes damage to your lungs, such as smoking. In smokers, the alveoli in the lungs can become damaged which interferes with the oxygen and carbon dioxide exchange. In severe cases of chronic pulmonary disease, you can see how some smokers' facial appearance changes. We used to call them blue bloaters and pink puffers and of course if they were unfortunate enough to catch Covid-19 with underlying lung damage the outlook is worse. You have now seen how important oxygen is and how important it is to preserve the atmosphere and environment and the planet.

If we do not protect the rainforests, we will have higher levels of carbon dioxide in the atmosphere. Carbon dioxide is a heat producing gas and there will be ozone layer depletion, causing global warming. The global temperature will rise and so will the sea level rise with it. The polar ice is melting with horrendous consequences. Some people in power do not believe in science and call it a hoax. As responsible citizens we should be asking them the question: without science, childhood vaccinations would not be there, protecting children from diphtheria, tetanus, whooping cough, meningitis, polio and many more diseases. Imagine if our leaders had called it a hoax and not allowed the vaccination of children, childhood vaccinations have saved more lives than anything else in the world. It is like saying, if we test more we will find more Coronavirus cases, we could apply the same principle and stop screening for cancers because we might find more cases and have to treat them? There is no logic in this argument. Imagine all the new technological advances in medical investigation and new treatments available saving millions of lives. It is up to us, the people, to believe either a scientist or a politician in power. I know who I would believe. We breathe in air which contains oxygen. It is equally important that we breathe air without pollution and toxic gases. Some industrial processes release harmful substances into the atmosphere. We have seen more than once in India how dangerous this can be. Recently a gas leak from the South Korean owned LG Chemicals killed twelve people and many more were injured. It is common knowledge, it was reported in media. In Bhopal, there was chemical contamination with horrendous consequences. What I am pointing at is how important it is to reduce the air pollution.

WATER

Water is an organic, transparent, tasteless, odourless and nearly colourless liquid which is the main constituent of Earth's Hydrosphere and fluid of most living organisms. It is vital to most life forms, even though it provides no calories or organic nutrients. Its chemical formula is H_2O, each of its molecules contains one oxygen and two hydrogen atoms. Water is the liquid state of H_2O and at a standard ambient temperature and pressure. It forms precipitation in the form of rain, aerosols in the form of fog and clouds are suspended droplets of water and ice. It is in a solid state when finely divided crystalline ice may precipitate to form snow. The gaseous state is water vapour or steam. Water moves continuously through the water cycle of evaporation, transpiration, condensation, precipitation and run off which reaches the sea. Water covers 71% of the Earth's surface and is mostly in seas and oceans. Approximately 70% of water used by humans goes into agriculture. We need water and without it we cannot survive more than three days. 60% of the adult human body is water, the brain and heart are composed of 73% water and the lungs about 83%. Skin contains 64% water, muscles and kidneys are 79% and even bones contain 31%.[1]

We cannot live without water. Yet there are parts of the world where none is readily available. In African countries we see charities raising money to provide drinking water for those communities. We need water in a pure form, contaminated water can spread waterborne diseases such as cholera, typhoid. Yet, even in countries like India, there are areas which don't have a proper water supply or sanitary facilities. According to the Forbes list, India has the third largest number of billionaires in the world, after the United States of America and China.

Nourishment

We all want to be healthy and happy and lead a good life. Of course, most of us manage but during a life time, occasionally some people will have problems with their health. From birth, the cells in our bodies are constantly multiplying and replacing worn out cells. It is surprising, even bone cells are replacing old bone and reforming new bone. Old bone cells are removed, and new bone is formed, these cells are called osteoclasts. They remove the old bone cells and then cells called osteogenic cells divide and form new bone. There are other bone cells called osteoblasts, they then become building blocks, but they cannot divide, and a matrix of calcium

---

[1] H. H. Mitchell, Journal of Biological Chemistry.

surrounds them, and these cells become mature osteocytes and that's how bone is formed but to perform this function properly they need the right materials, protein, calcium, phosphates, minerals and vitamins and oxygen. You can see the problem and how things can go wrong.

Stem cells are embryonic cells, they can become any cell in the body. However, once these cells mature, they become specialised in function like liver cells, brain cells, heart muscle cells and kidney cells, etc. Each cell has a special function, and all the cells work together to form an organ like a liver, kidney, heart to function efficiently.

Another example are red blood cells called erythrocytes. They are formed in bone marrow and their main function is carrying oxygen from the lungs around the whole body. Red blood cells contain a substance called haemoglobin. I have already explained how they carry oxygen. The red blood cell has a lifespan of one hundred and twenty days and will be replaced by new cells manufactured in the bone marrow. To form new red blood cells there needs to be the right materials: a protein, iron, oxygen, water, fat and vitamins. If we fail to provide this then there won't be any healthy red blood cells, but abnormal cell formation. Oxygen will not be supplied to the vital organs. When you have an iron deficiency, you can become short of breath and tired because you are not getting enough oxygen. This is the same with all organs like the kidneys, liver, heart, brain, they won't be able to function efficiently.

I am going to describe how to get this right if we can prevent problems happening. We have already discussed about oxygen, water and now we need to look at the other ingredients, food. We need to eat foods to provide these ingredients. Protein, fats and carbohydrates are important, they are the main components of almost all cells. Vitamins and minerals are also required but how do we get them and what from which foods?

PROTEIN — Meat is a good source of protein.

The following are some of the meats and their protein content:

Skinless and boneless chicken has 22.5 g/100 g.

Lamb loin chops have 20.9 g/100 g.

Large hamburger patty has 16.5 g/100g

Meats also contain fat and are easy to digest compared to vegetarian proteins. Another advantage of beef and steak is that they also contain iron, but we do know regular consumption of red meat increases the risk of certain cancers by 20%. I would suggest one or twice a week is fine.

For vegetarians, there are plenty of options and it is much safer and cheaper and is more environmentally friendly, as well as having a lower risk of cancer. I very rarely eat red meat, although I used to in my younger days. Of course, it is a matter of personal choice but all the evidence I have seen over my GP days is in favour of the vegetarian diet, maybe that's my Hindu bias. The following suggestions are vegetarian sources of protein:

SOYA BEANS — These contain 36.5 grams of protein per 100 grams.

Soya beans are also a source of 8 essential amino acids, and I will explain later on what these amino acids do and why they are important. Soya beans are higher in fat than other legumes, however it is mainly good mono-unsaturated and poly-unsaturated fats, including omega 3 fatty acids. They are also a good source of calcium, iron and magnesium. I am very fond of soya beans, I have soya milk and yogurt daily and once or twice a week, tofu. I think it's an excellent food for health but, of course, I would not suggest you have to eat tofu every day.

CHEESE — is a high source of protein with 35.8 g per 100 grams. It is also a good source of vitamin A and calcium but also a high sodium and fat content. Therefore, we may have it once a twice a week and that will be enough to provide the required protein.

HEMP SEEDS — have 31.6 g per 100 grams and it contains both omega 3 and omega 6 fatty acids and a rich source of magnesium, zinc and phosphorus. These seeds are a nutritional powerhouse, they are related to the cannabis plant, but you do not get high on them. They seem to have no side-effects and you get them in health food shops.

PUMPKIN SEEDS — contain 30.2 g per 100 grams and have high levels of magnesium, L-tryptophan which improves the mood naturally and phosphorus which are supposed to reduce the level of LDL cholesterol which is a bad cholesterol. They also known to improve the condition of skin.

PEANUTS — have 25.8 g per 100 grams and are a great source of magnesium. They are a cheaper source of protein but contain saturated fat. Eating them every now and then is acceptable as an alternative source of protein. This is my weakness I seem to eat more than I should.

WHEAT PROTEIN — this is made from wheat gluten and has more protein and can be made into many meatless options. There is almost no fat or cholesterol but if you are sensitive to gluten it is not an option for you to try.

LENTILS — are another of my favourites and contain 24.6 g per 100grams. Lentils are very good for a vegetarian diet as they are cholesterol free, high in fibre, low in fat and sodium. Lentils have a high amount of thiamine, vitamin B1 and folate.

KIDNEY BEANS — contain 24.4 g per 100 grams and contain iron and a high amount of fibre. They are good for people with diabetes.

GREEN BEANS — have a protein content of 23.8 grams per 100 grams and they are low in fat and sodium but high in fibre. They also contain antioxidants, lutein and zeaxanthin, which are supposed to be good for your eyes. They also have vitamin C which is an antioxidant and prevents scurvy. There are a number of other beans which have high fibre contents.

ALMONDS — contain 21.1 grams per 100 grams and high amounts of vitamin B2 and is an excellent source of vitamin E.

SUNFLOWER SEEDS — contain 28.8 g per 100 grams and are the richest source of vitamin E. This vitamin is an antioxidant and helps protect against cell damage. They also contain high levels of copper which helps your skin. Sunflower seeds are extremely high in vitamins B1 and B6. I would certainly recommend these at least once or twice a week

CASHEW NUTS — contain 18.2 g per 100 grams and they are rich in zinc, copper and magnesium but they are also high in fat.

MYCOPROTEIN (QUORN) — contains 15.2 g per 100 grams and has become a very popular part of a vegetarian diet as it has a texture like meat and has no trans-fats which are bad fats and is convenient.

WILD RICE — contains 14.7 g per 100 grams and it is high in fibre, magnesium, phosphorus and zinc.

BASMATI RICE — contains 3.54 grams of protein per 100 grams and a high amount of carbohydrate at 25.22 grams per hundred gram and 121 kcal. However, if you prefer the taste it is okay but for healthy diet I feel it is not the best rice, whole grain is better although calories are similar but has 1 percent requirement of fibre.

I think I have compiled what I consider to be a healthy, vegetarian alternatives for meat but those who like meat they have that choice as well.

ESSENTIAL AMINO-ACIDS

There are nine amino-acids which the body cannot make, so they must come from food. For vegetarians it comes from soya, quinoa, buck wheat, eggs and milk and for non-vegetarians it comes from meat, chicken and seafood. We need these essential amino acids for protein synthesis, hormone synthesis and neurotransmitter production, these are involved in the mood changes. For those who like fish, it is a good source of protein, omega 3 fatty acids and vitamin D.

I would prefer deep sea fish like tuna, it is less likely to be contaminated with toxins. Salmon is another option but personally, I do not recommend shellfish because they can be contaminated with toxins and more likely to be high in uric acid. If you have gout or a similar condition, I think you should avoid it but if you just fancy it once in a while there is no harm as the body will cope with it.

FATS

The body requires fat. It is one of the essential components of cell walls and hormones. The fat-soluble vitamins: A, D, E and K cannot be absorbed without fat. Sources of fat for non-vegetarians are meat, eggs, fish. Meat has high amounts of unsaturated fat, and which is not good for health. Therefore, consumption should be reduced to once or twice a week. For vegetarians, cheese and butter provide fats but these are saturated fats which are not as good for you, as unsaturated fats, so keep it to a minimum. It is best to eat mono-unsaturated fats to maintain high levels of HDL (high density lipoprotein) cholesterol and reduce LDL (low density lipoprotein) cholesterol. A good source of this is olive oil, I use extra-virgin olive oil even for cooking, but it is not suitable for deep frying as it has a lower ignition point than other oils. Rapeseed oil and avocados are another good source and the total cholesterol/HDL ratio below 6 and the LDL cholesterol below 3.00mmol/L. In general, anything above 2 for HDL Cholesterol is good and this can be improved by exercise

All the foods for both vegetarian and non-vegetarians should have essential fatty acids and foods like fish and soya beans, walnuts, chai seeds and flaxseeds have been good source.

People always ask about cholesterol, let me explain all about cholesterol, good and bad. High-density lipoprotein is HDL-cholesterol, triglycerides, and low-density lipoprotein is LDL-cholesterol. Serum cholesterol/HDL ratio.

So why do we worry about cholesterol? The reason is LDL-cholesterol transports cholesterol around the body to produce hormones and make new cell membranes. It deposits excess cholesterol in the walls lining the arteries where there is damage. Such damage, or more correctly inflammation is caused by the chemicals in smoking, and the wear and tear high blood pressure has on the vessels. High levels of cholesterol also have an abrasive action on the lining of blood vessels. When the LDL-cholesterol deposits excess cholesterol at these sites, it starts to build up and form plaques, leading to narrowing and blockages in the arteries of the heart, brain, kidneys and legs. This can lead to heart attacks, strokes and peripheral vascular disease in the legs. In severe cases of peripheral vascular disease, a leg may become ischaemic (die due to lack of oxygen) and have to be amputated. I have had to deal with this on occasion when I was working in surgery. I remember having to perform leg amputations, fortunately nowadays it is usually diagnosed early, and the risk of amputation is low.

HDL-cholesterol is a good cholesterol and the higher its level the better. It works removing excess circulating cholesterol and returning it to the liver for re-processing. It improves with exercise. All I can say is, avoid a diet high in LDL-cholesterol and do at least moderate exercise, even a 20 minute walk can make a difference if done regularly and can increase HDL-Cholesterol to keep you healthier.

Now we need to look at other parts of our food and that is carbohydrates:

CARBOHYDRATES — Carbohydrates are broken down in the body into glucose which our cells use for energy. The brain is the most sensitive organ in the body to low glucose. Which are the best carbohydrates for health? I think those are the ones which are closest to nature as possible. Vegetables, fruit, pulses, legumes, unsweetened dairy products and 100% whole-grains, like brown rice, quinoa, wheat and oats.

For the average British adult male requires 2500 calories a day and adult female requires 2000 calories a day. Ideally, we should get 45-65% of our calories from carbohydrates, 10-30% from proteins and 28-35% from fats.

To calculate calories, we need to know the calorific value of 1 gram of each:

1 gram of protein has 4 calories

1 gram fat has 8 calories

1 gram of carbohydrate has 4 calories.

Now we can calculate how much of each of these foods we can eat.

VITAMINS

Vitamins are very important to health and well-being. The following are water soluble vitamins which do not require fat for absorption:

1. B1, thiamine
2. B2, riboflavin
3. B3, niacin (nicotinic acid)
4. B5, pantothenic acid
5. B6, pyridoxine
6. B7, biotin
7. B9, folate (folic acid)
8. B12, cyanocobalamin (cobalamin)
9. C, ascorbic acid

There are also fat-soluble vitamins which can only be absorbed if there is fat present in the diet. These are A, D, E and K. We need these vitamins because most of the vitamins act as co-enzymes, these are non-protein compounds that bind with enzyme to catalyse reactions for the metabolic processes in the body. Multivitamins can be used in a balanced diet, but some are difficult especially if you are vegan. Another thing I should point out, vitamin B1 is inhibited by drinking alcohol. This is why people who are alcoholic may need a vitamin B1 supplement.

On one of Captain James Cook's voyages, scurvy (vitamin C deficiency) developed amongst his ship's crew. I think it was his first voyage on the HMS Endeavour. Subsequently he found out how to treat and prevent scurvy with vitamin C. He did not know at the time it was vitamin C deficiency, but he did know what helped and used a variety of different fruits and sour kraut (pickled cabbage). We rarely see scurvy anymore and I do not recall seeing anyone with scurvy in general practice. Citrus fruits such as oranges, lemons and green leafy vegetables are a good source of vitamin C. It is an excellent antioxidant.

MINERALS

Minerals are elements that are needed by the body to function normally, for example phosphorus is important for healthy bones and teeth and I have already stated which foods contain phosphorus. Magnesium is also used in bones.

SULPHUR — is chemical element with symbol S and atomic number 16. It is abundant, multivalent and non-metallic. Under normal conditions, sulphur atoms form atomic molecules with a chemical formula S8. Elemental sulphur is a bright yellow, crystalline solid at room temperature. Sulphur is essential for life because it is part of many amino acids and vitamins.

IRON — Iron is important for the formation of healthy red blood cells. In haemoglobin, iron in the form of haem transports oxygen around the body. It is readily available in meat, egg yolks and green leafy vegetables. If taken with vitamin C or food containing vitamin C it will be absorbed better.

IODINE is used by the thyroid hormone. Thyroid hormones are essential for metabolism of food to produce energy. You may remember seeing a goitre, a swelling in the neck due to the thyroid gland enlargement. This is due to a deficiency of iodine, the thyroid gland enlarges in an attempt to produce enough thyroxine. Iodine is now added to salt.

Goitres were common in Derbyshire, back in the day and known as "Derbyshire Neck".

SELENIUM, COPPER and FLUORIDE are also required for good health.

What I know is that if you have a well-balanced diet and variety in what you eat, most of us will get the necessary elements. I have given plenty of suggestions with regards to food for vegetarians and non-vegetarians and what I would like to add is fresh fruits and green leafy vegetables are the most important part of diet.

Mind, Body and Spirit

EXERCISE

Almost all of us know that exercise is beneficial to us. Benefits can be seen even with a moderate amount of exercise, such as walking twenty minutes a day. There are variety of ways you can exercise, and people can choose what suits them best for their needs and liking.

Walking is very common, and this is one of my favourite hobbies. When I was in medical school I used to run, cycle and played physical sports like volleyball, badminton, tennis and an Indian game called kabbadi. During my last few years in General Practice, then more so after I retired, I took up walking. On the 11th of August 2016 I was very stressed and could not concentrate. I became very forgetful and started to feel very low. I decided to start walking as a regular hobby. I realised I was not as fit as I thought and was getting short of breath and tired even after walking just two km on flat ground, but I continued and after a while I felt more comfortable, less tired. I increased my walking distance to four km and in one month as was feeling fine. Then I started to do some uphill walks as well and I was fine too. My concentration, forgetfulness and mood all improved and since then I have walked a minimum of seven km every single day, which is approximately ten thousand steps a day. My average speed is fifteen minutes per kilometre. Between of the 11th of August

2016 and 15th of November 2020, I have walked fifteen thousand km, I recorded my progress every day on my calendar. I find walking easy, you do not need any preparation, all you need is to put on shoes and maybe a coat and walk. I walk anywhere, in the house, the garden and you do not have to do it all in one go. You can do it in short bursts, in fact I have walked in airports from one end to the other of the terminals and it gives me an easy thirty minutes exercise. I walk on holidays on the beaches, and hotels, in the room and it's a hobby I enjoy. I am not asking everyone else to follow me but even if you can do twenty minutes a day it helps maintain fitness. One positive thing I must mention, you can walk even at a good old age as long as you can put one foot in front of the other. I will continue as long as I can, but in time I might have to do less, and I am aware of it. Recently I bumped into the urology consultant I used to work for. He used to run miles. Sadly, now in his eighties he had a stroke. I met him out walking, his wife supporting him. He was pleased to stop and chat and told me his wife made sure he kept walking, and it had improved his balance and general health. I sometimes walk eighteen km a day but that is the maximum I have done. Rain, snow, wind, nothing stops me, even a cough or cold. I know some people think I do too much, but what is too much? Some people prefer to go to the gym to do strenuous exercise and that's good for them. There is no problem with that as it is exercise and that's what matters but not everyone is fit enough. One problem with the gym is you have to pay. Another good exercise is cycling but I find it difficult because you have to prepare to go cycling and the roads are quite busy, but my neighbours ride regularly and they enjoy it. Cycling can be quite strenuous and sometimes it can cause prostate damage due to friction.

Swimming is my second favourite form of exercise, it's passive exercise and kinder on the joints. I usually swim when I'm on holiday both in the pool and the sea, but one disadvantage is not many people have swimming pools at home and you have to pay as well so it's not for everybody.

What I would recommend is that you choose what you like and what you are capable of doing. Exercise certainly helped me, I have been walking for more than four years and I am happy with it. The advantages can include weight loss, prevention of diabetes, strokes and heart attacks. It improves your thinking and is known to improve your mood through the release of endorphins, the "feel good" hormones, it also improves your co-ordination.

Religion and Spirituality

How does your mind control your body? To some degree you can explain knowing the functions of the brain in a scientific way, but not all. There must be other reasons we do not know about. Religious people believe there is a God, and He is totally responsible for our being here and the God has total control of our lives. It does not matter what religion, as almost all religions believe in God and His power and it has been a belief for thousands of years, all over the world. So, there must be some truth in it, but scientists argue and look for proof.

I have one question for scientists and that is when a woman gets pregnant, at twenty-two days after conception the baby's heart starts beating and the beat starts at a specialised a group of cells called the sinoatrial node. This node is situated at the right atrium at the junction of the superior vena cava (main vein in the body). This creates an electrical impulse which spreads across the whole heart and makes the cardiac muscle fibres contract and the heart pumps blood around the circulatory system. At five weeks, at the earliest we can hear the beat on an ultrasound scan. This beating process continues every second, every minute, twenty-four hours a day, seven days a week without any rest and continues throughout our life, it does not matter how long you live but one day it will stop. It does not matter how pure the air you are breathing is, it doesn't matter how healthy your diet is and it does not matter how much exercise you take, the heart will stop beating. I have never seen or heard or read about anyone living forever. So, my first question is what makes the heart start beating spontaneously? The second question is why does it stop at a certain point? I do not think there is an answer, and this is why I think there must be something beyond what we know.

I was brought up in a Hindu family and as a child I used to go to Temple and walk the twenty-one circles around the temple of Hanuman, circling clockwise and praying as I went. If I remember correctly, I will ask God to give me good health, peace and love and help me give aid to others who were in need. This left me feeling very happy and content, but when I went away to school, I lost that habit. No one ever questioned me about it, I was left to decide what's best for me. I have already talked about my very interesting experiences as a child. These experiences left deep impressions on my mind, and maybe I think there must be something beyond that we cannot comprehend, that, I believe it strongly. I also believe in fate. I find it difficult to understand when people condemn religion and religious beliefs. When I was working at Guy's hospital, the consultant neurosurgeon with a western qualification, FRCS, looked straight into my eyes and told me

I will never become a FRCS. Who do you believe, the man without any education who looked straight into my eyes and told me my future or the western educated man who told me I would never gain a FRCS. I did become a Fellow of the Royal College of Surgeons. As far as I am concerned, if religious people want to follow their beliefs and pray, they can do as they wish as long as it does no harm to anybody. What I do not accept is killing innocent people in the name of religion. I have a lot of experience dealing people with different religious beliefs. As a doctor I treated a large number of Christian patients and a fairly large number of Muslim patients and some Jewish, Hindu and Buddhists. I found them all equally respectable people. Our local vicar and his wife are a shining example of honesty, integrity and caring to all parts of our society. I never found them to discriminate against anybody and I think they followed a true religion. The only time I have had a problem with religion is when people use religion as a political tool to create hatred and division.

In my own life, I follow my own principle as part of my religion, treat people with respect and dignity and do no harm. I married Heather, my wife, who is Christian, and she felt that both our children should be christened into the Church of England. I had no problems with that because as they grow up they can make their own choices as to who they want to be, as long as they are decent human beings.

Prejudice

One evening, we were having a meal at Dick Hudsons restaurant near Ilkley in Yorkshire. I like this place and I have been a number of times with Heather's parents. It is situated on the moors. This time we went because Heather and her cousins had organised a family history weekend. Just before the meal we were having a drink and one of Heather's relatives, asked me a question that concerned her friend, an Anglo-Indian lady whom she really liked. This lady had said she had suffered from racial prejudice in her life, and did I have any problems? This was a fair question but her daughter, who is one of the nicest people, was quite embarrassed by the questioning I think, but I was not. I thought it was a fair question and I just said yes but nothing I could not deal with, and I said there is prejudice in every society, that includes my country of birth. When I went to India, with Heather, a Hindu friend, a member of the legislative assembly for Maharashtra who was my friends brother in-law asked me how I felt about marrying a Christian girl and abandoning my Hindu religion. My reply was straightforward and honest. I treat all people with respect and dignity, irrespective of their religion, colour of skin or sex and as far as I understand the Hindu religion does not discriminate and has similar principles. He did not say anything further, but Heather's relative did have a profound effect on my thinking. Although I never liked to play the racial card because I know better. There are decent people in every society and of course the small minority for whatever reason develop hate for people with different skin colour, sex, age or whatever.

I have therefore decided to write my own experience but that does not reflect on the best part of the British society because I know most British people are not like this. I am going to write just a couple of instances of what I call prejudice.

One day, Heather and I went shopping at Curries. We parked, got out and walked towards the shop. A man, probably in his twenties was walking past with his parents and partner. Without any reason he just walked towards me but was probably twenty feet away and just shouted, 'Hey, you Paki!' I looked around to see if he was shouting at someone else, there was nobody. I have never ever had this said to me before and I was so shocked I walked straight towards him and pointed a finger in his face, not quite touching him!

'How do you know where I come from?' I said, and even before he could answer, I said, 'You have very few brain cells in your thick skull and you don't have a clue, you said this because of the colour of my skin and the next time you call me this—' I cannot repeat what said! I still do not know what gave me the courage to say this, his parents, girlfriend and Heather were all shocked by my reaction. He just walked away, and I could hear his parents telling him off. I must point out I am not a violent person, and this was very out of character for me.

Another incident I remember was when I was at home. We have been fortunate that we have very good neighbours, and I cannot ever remember having cross words with any of them. We really get on well. One day, one of the neighbours had someone to do some work in his house. I knew this particular neighbour and he is very meticulous so if anybody does work for him, they have to be good. We needed a new kitchen fitting, so I thought I would ask this guy because he must be good. I spoke to him and took his telephone number and asked him if he could do our kitchen, he said give him a call. One evening after work, at about seven p.m., I rang and to my surprise he got really abusive and started using racist language, before I could say anything he put the phone down. He was from Barnoldswick, not far from us. I checked the number and address were correct. I was shocked, the next day I rang the police and told them exactly what happened. They were very thorough and sympathetic and said they would investigate and be in touch with me. Of course, they did their job, visited and interviewed him. He accepted it was him and said he was very sorry, he did not know why he said what he said and apologised to the police. He said his brother-in-law was Afro-Caribbean and he was not racist. The police rang me and asked if I am happy to accept the apology and drop the case or they could take it further if I wanted? I said no, that was satisfactory I did not want to take it any further and I thanked them for their help.

What I learnt from this was, yes, I was in a privileged position as a doctor, and I could get some justice but what happens to the thousands of ordinary people who have no support. It should not be like this, it does not matter who you are.

Democracy

You might wonder as a doctor why I am writing about Democracy, and I would like to explain my reasons.

First and foremost, health and equality depend on the principles of democracy. I came to the United Kingdom in 1973 and made my home here, I liked the democracy and human rights. In my eyes the United Kingdom has been one of the oldest and finest democracies in the world but in the last few years it has changed. If I am concerned about it then I should use my democratic right and express my view. I will start from the beginning of how democracy started.

Democracy is derived from the Greek words demokratia, demos (people) and cratos (rules), rule by the people. In this form of government, people have the authority to choose the government making legislation, who the people are and how the authority is shared among them. The core issues of the democratic theory are development and constitution. Some considerations of these issues are freedom of assembly and speech, inclusiveness and equality, membership, consent, voting, the right to life and minority rights.

Generally, there are two types of democracies:

Direct democracy — where the people directly deliberate and decide on legislature.

Representative democracy — which is where the people elect representatives to deliberate and decide on legislature, such as in parliament or presidential democracy.

Liquid democracy — combines elements of these two basic types.

However, the democracy has overtime been modified by more than three thousand and five hundred adjectives, this means it has changed a lot

The most common today, a decision-making approach of democracy has been the majority rule in some countries, notably the United Kingdom, which originated the Westminster system. The dominant principle is that of the Parliamentary sovereignty while maintaining judicial independence. In the United States, separation of power is often cited as a central attribute. Athenians established what is generally considered to be the first democracy in 508–507 BC. Cleisthenes is referred to as the father of Athenian democracy.

British democracy — Magna Carta Libertatum — this is Latin for the Great Charter for Freedom, more commonly called the Magna Carta, the great charter. It was the charter of rights agreed by King John at Runnymede near Windsor on the 15th of June 1215. It was first drafted by the Archbishop of Canterbury to make peace between the unpopular King John of England and the group of rebel barons. It promised protection of church rights and protection for the barons from illegal imprisonment, access to swift justice and limitations on the feudal payments to the crown to be implemented through a council of twenty-five barons. Neither side had stood behind their commitments and the charter was annulled by Pope Innocent III, leading to the first barons' war.

The British democracy is one of the oldest democracies in the world. Although the Magna Carta was the beginning, full democracy was established much later. David Cameron was asked a question about the Magna Carta on his visit to America in 2012, he did not know the meaning, of course, he had an advantage because of his upbringing, and it helped him to get where he wanted to go. Over the centuries it has changed, but the fundamental principle remains the same as Parliamentary democracy. Lately it has changed so much, one wonders what the value of democracy is.

In the last few years, the country has become divided more than ever and of course, it has created a lot of anger in millions of people. This is not going to help anybody. As long as we have a party-political system in place, we are always going to be divided like the blue, red, green party and any other colours of the various parties. Added to that, rich millionaires on one side and working-class people and unions on the other and on top of that the foreign influence in party politics.

Winston Churchill said, 'democracy is the worst form of Government, except for all those other forms of Government that have been tried from time to time.'

At this present time, I for one totally agree with his first part but I disagree with the second. Under the present circumstances, how do we unite the nation which is so divided? People are voting for the party, not the person generally. Even though he or she may not have the talent to represent the people, people have been elected simply because they belong to particular party. As long they are loyal to their party leader and follow his or her orders.

The independent mind is not allowed to flourish and that is why so many MPs are not of a higher calibre. This applies to all parties, we are not giving chances to real, honest, hard-working and independent minded people. That means we lose some of the value of democracy.

My suggestion is to abolish the political party system and allow all members of Parliament to stand independently for the Parliament elected from each Parliamentary area. Money for the election should come from the government. The national independent executive bodies which oversee the election, and all independent MPs then elect the Prime Minister. There will be no influence from unions, there will be no influence by foreign donors or foreign governments. It will be called a government of national unity. This process can be used for council elections too.

People will say, well our democracy is the oldest in the world and tried and tested system, why should we change? My question is why not unless you try you do not know. I can see there will be opposition from all parties, but it cannot be worse than what we have now. So much energy is being wasted by hating each other, dividing neighbourhoods and even families. It's worth a try to bring some decency, humanity and equality in the country, and this is where my journey had brought me.

The Journey So Far...

I have had a long but very satisfying journey, first through India's young democracy and then through the well-established British democracy. Along the way I had some wonderful times, there were some ups and downs, but I have no regrets. I have a wonderful family and friends too. During my journey I travelled the length and breadth of Great Britain, from Scotland to South Wales, then London to Scotland and Stafford to North Wales and then to Blackburn and Lincoln, over to Liverpool and finally back to Blackburn, now I also spend time in Greater Manchester.

Along the way I met so many decent people who helped me progress through my career and I have accumulated a wealth of memories and those will remain with me forever.

As I have written already, I met some wonderful staff and patients who made me who I am, and I am very grateful to them.

I thoroughly enjoyed writing my journey and if you enjoy reading as much I did writing, it's worthwhile.

Printed in Great Britain
by Amazon

81834329R00161